BUSINESS PLANS THAT WIN $$$

BUSINESS PLANS THAT WIN $$$

LESSONS FROM THE
MIT ENTERPRISE FORUM^{SM}

Stanley R. Rich and David E. Gumpert

HARPER & ROW, PUBLISHERS, New York

Cambridge, Philadelphia, San Francisco, London

1817 *Mexico City, São Paulo, Singapore, Sydney*

BUSINESS PLANS THAT WIN $$$. Copyright © 1985 by Stanley R. Rich and David E. Gumpert. All rights reserved. Printed in the United States of America. No part of this book may be used or reproduced in any manner whatsoever without written permission except in the case of brief quotations embodied in critical articles and reviews. For information address Harper & Row, Publishers, Inc., 10 East 53rd Street, New York, N.Y. 10022. Published simultaneously in Canada by Fitzhenry & Whiteside Limited, Toronto.

FIRST EDITION

Designer: Sidney Feinberg

Library of Congress Cataloging in Publication Data

Rich, Stanley R.
  Business plans that win $$$.

  Includes index.
  1. New business enterprises—Finance.
I. Gumpert, David E.   II. Title.
HG4027.6.R53   1985   658.1'5   84-48617
ISBN 0-06-015439-X

---

85 86 87 88 89 10 9 8 7 6 5 4 3 2 1

For our Wives,
Shirley C. Rich and Jean S. Gumpert

Contents

This book is designed to provide authoritative information about preparing a business plan. It is sold with the understanding that plans created in accordance with the principles herein are not guaranteed to win funding.

In the interest of protecting the privacy of individuals whose real identities are not central to the examples of business plans given in this book, names and other descriptive details have been altered where examples have been provided.

Preface

How can you prepare a business plan that will have the greatest appeal to investors—that will win the investment dollars necessary to help you create a successful business? What do investors look for—and look out for—in any business plan? What should you emphasize? What should you play down? And how should you package the plan for greatest effect?

Business Plans That Win $$$ offers answers to these and other questions from the perspective of professional investors. Their do's and don'ts have not been a part of the many other manuals and textbooks on business plan preparation. Here are the strong opinions of investors, backed by explanations and case histories, showing why, for example, your business must be perceived as "market-driven" rather than "product-driven" and how you can create this perception in the business plan.

You can also use this book to gain insight into how investors evaluate young companies. To aid in understanding the evaluation process, we introduce a new rating system that predicts which types of enterprises are most desirable to investors and which are unlikely to win funding.

You will be introduced as well to the thought processes and formulas that determine how much of the company the investor must receive in return for the investment. And you will explore the issue of how the investor can cash out of the investment in three to seven years with appropriate capital appreciation, and how much that must be to justify the investment.

In addition to serving as a guidebook for preparing business plans, this book has a broader and more long-term purpose: to encourage a process of education and planning that will orient entrepreneurs toward the steps necessary to achieve company excellence—and profitability.

The process of starting a business and managing it through its formative years has traditionally been thought to be chaotic, defying logic and order. But that thinking has undergone major changes. Those of us who watch and work with emerging enterprises have long felt that the successful birth and nurturing of ventures isn't simply a matter of chance and luck.

Peter Drucker took note of this change in thinking in his 1984 *Harvard Business Review* article about the evolving importance of young businesses in the American economy. "Although it has become fashionable to contrast a supposedly obsolete 'managerial' era of the past with a triumphantly emerging 'entrepreneurial' era, it makes better sense to see in this flowering of an entrepreneurial economy the triumph of systematic management."

Our source for much of this information is investor evaluations of business plans at MIT Enterprise Forum℠ sessions (described beginning on page xiii); the Forum's ongoing programs to assist new and emerging companies are in the forefront of the efforts to apply existing management principles to the entrepreneurial drive that Mr. Drucker alludes to. This book is an extension of the Enterprise Forum's effort to systematize the planning process for new and emerging enterprises. Indeed, we hope you find this book useful as a formulation of guiding principles to govern the planning process for young ventures.

One caution: This is not a book of forms. We believe strongly that the process of assembling a business plan is in significant measure a process of chronicling the market evaluation, people mobilization, product or service development, and other efforts that are at the heart of building a business. It is also a process of making decisions and projections based on progress to date. To view business-plan preparation as merely a writing assignment is to seriously misjudge the nature of the task at hand.

In line with that thinking, we bemoan the efforts of some consultants to develop model business plans, which can then be prepared for individual clients simply by filling in a few blanks. We are convinced that individual businesses always differ enough that to attempt to fit them all into a common cookie-cutter format is ridiculous and risks glossing over important individual issues and giving undue emphasis to minor subjects.

We have thus resisted the temptation to include "sample" business plans. Since there is no one "right" way to formulate the plan's language and assertions, we concluded that to excerpt from business plans would only confuse and mislead.

Nevertheless, in identifying the principles which we believe guide the investment process, we have sought to be specific. We both explain these principles and offer suggestions for complying, whatever your own situation may be. Please keep in mind, however, that the process of identifying ventures in which to invest is a far from perfect one.

Certain of our ideas may meet with disagreement from some in the investment community. But such is the nature of books which seek to formulate ideas that beforehand were mostly expressed verbally and incompletely.

Using opinion and fact, then, this book distills many years of our experience. Stanley Rich has founded, funded, operated, and sold seven technology-based businesses over a thirty-five-year period. He has prepared and evaluated hundreds of business plans in his role as entrepreneur and chairman of the MIT Enterprise Forum, which he co-founded. David Gumpert has helped write and evaluate many business plans and has been involved in researching the managerial challenges of emerging companies in his role as small business editor of the *Harvard Business Review.*

The MIT Enterprise Forum is oriented heavily toward encouraging and assisting fast-growth companies seeking investment funds. Because we have based our book extensively on cases entrepreneurs bring before the Enterprise Forum for counsel and guidance, our emphasis is on founders' desire for investment capital to aid their companies in achieving substantial growth.

That doesn't mean that the principles here don't apply to many others, such as business people seeking bank loans or other debt financing who will improve their chances of obtaining funding by having a credible business plan.

Corporate managers who are proposing new projects and products or expanding divisions must also frequently assemble convincing business plans. This book's ideas can be applied to the preparation of such corporate documents.

Finally, we hope this book will be of value to consultants, bankers, venture capitalists, and others who must deal with entrepreneurs. At a minimum, it should aid these professionals in evaluating the higher quality business plans that will inevitably result from all the entrepreneurs who apply this book's principles.

About the MIT Enterprise Forum^{SM}

The MIT Enterprise Forum^{SM} is a national clinic for providing assistance to emerging growth companies. Organized under the auspices of the Massachusetts Institute of Technology Alumni Association in 1978, it offers businesses at a critical stage of development an opportunity to obtain counsel from a panel of alumni experts and others on possible steps to take to achieve their goals.

Its main activity consists of monthly evening sessions in which the business plans of companies accepted for presentation are evaluated during sixty- to ninety-minute "no-holds-barred" sessions. The format allows the presenter or presenters twenty minutes to summarize their business plan orally. Then each of four panelists—venture capitalists, bankers, marketing specialists, successful entrepreneurs, professors, and other experts—spends five to ten minutes each giving his assessments of the strengths and weaknesses of the plan and the enterprise and suggestions for improvement. (Each panelist reviews the written business plan in advance of the sessions.)

In some cases, the panelists suggest a completely new direction. In others, they advise on more effectively carrying out existing policies. Their comments range over the entire spectrum of business issues.

Following the panelists' evaluations, audience members can ask questions and offer comments. Sessions are open to the public and typically draw about three hundred people, most of them financiers, business executives, accountants, lawyers, consultants, and others with special interests in emerging companies.

Presenters have the opportunity to respond to the evaluations and suggestions offered. They also receive written evaluations of the oral presentation from audience members. (The written plan isn't made available to the audience.) These monthly sessions are held primarily for companies that have advanced beyond the startup stage—they tend to be from one to ten years old—and are in need of specialized advice.

The MIT Enterprise Forum^{SM} in Cambridge, Massachusetts, is overseen by its executive committee, comprised of experienced business executives who donate their time and services to the Forum (as do panelists). These executives include entrepreneurs, financiers, bankers, consultants, and professors from the Massachusetts Institute of Technology and Harvard Business Schools.

In addition to the regular monthly case sessions, the MIT Enterprise Forum sponsors a Startup Clinic every other month at which entrepreneurs seeking advice and funds for beginning enterprises make presentations. The Startup Clinic is a more loosely structured event and is open to only about forty entrepreneurs, small business professionals, consultants, investors, and others who might be of direct assistance to the startup enterprises.

The monthly MIT Enterprise Forum sessions have heard business-plan presentations from more than one hundred companies. The Startup Clinic has had more than fifty presentations. The executive committee has reviewed hundreds of business plans and counseled many of the founders outside the confines of the formal Enterprise Forum sessions.

Many companies have received financing after their founders have made presentations at Enterprise Forum sessions. Regardless of whether they receive funding, the entrepreneurs typically say they have benefited greatly from the sessions.

The MIT Enterprise Forum also publishes a monthly newsletter (*The Forum Reporter*) and presents annual day-long workshops on a critical aspect of technology-based small business; workshops have addressed business-plan preparation, the selling of technology-based companies, marketing, and other issues.

The MIT Enterprise Forum's success in Cambridge has led MIT alumni and business leaders to establish Forums in other cities in the United States. MIT Enterprise Forums now exist in New York, Washington/Baltimore, Houston, Chicago, Denver, Seattle, Miami, and Los Angeles. Others are being planned in Philadelphia, Hartford, Minneapolis, Dallas, San Diego, and Stamford, Connecticut. An experimentor Forum was held in Holland, and other potential ones are being discussed in Mexico City, Berlin, Toronto, and London. A complete list follows at the end of this book.

Although we rely heavily on the Forum's principles and information, the ideas expressed here are those of the authors and do not necessarily reflect the views of the MIT Enterprise Forum^{SM}.

Acknowledgments

This book benefited enormously from the generous input and support of many individuals.

We are especially grateful to several officials of the Massachusetts Institute of Technology, the MIT Enterprise Forum, and the *Harvard Business Review*. These include Vincent A. Fulmer, secretary of MIT, William J. Hecht, executive vice president of the MIT Alumni Association, Paul E. Johnson, national director of the MIT Enterprise Forum, and Kenneth R. Andrews, editor of the *Harvard Business Review*.

In addition, we were fortunate enough to have had the help of a few expert and dedicated individuals who assisted us in transcribing, editing, and organizing our notes and drafts. Julie Fernandez, a former *Harvard Business Review* manuscript editor, and Leonore J. Gumpert, a veteran editorial assistant, aided us in our transcribing efforts. Stephanie Zurmuhlen, a Babson College student, made important contributions in editing and organizing material.

We must not neglect to mention the important contributions and cooperation of the MIT Enterprise Forum executive committee. Its members include Russell N. Cox, Robert J. Crowley, Vincent A. Fulmer, Paul M. Kelley, Aaron Kleiner, Peter J. Lazarkis, Robert C. McCray, Richard C. Munn, Judith H. Obermayer, John F. O'Donnell, Rajeshwari Patel,

Arthur C. Parthe Jr., Edward B. Roberts, Jerome J. Schaufeld, Howard H. Stevenson, and Barry Unger.

Finally, we wish to thank two individuals who believed in this book from very early on. Harriet Rubin, our editor at Harper & Row, not only encouraged us to write this book when it was only a germ of an idea, but made important and sensitive editorial contributions as we developed the manuscript. And Philippa Brophy, our agent at The Sterling Lord Agency, was extraordinary in her patience and persistence in seeing the project through to completion.

1

What Investors Look For —And Look Out For

The business plan is the ticket of admission to the investment process. Without a plan, furnished in advance, many investor groups won't even grant an interview. And the plan must be outstanding if it is to win investment funds.

Entrepreneurs can be easily tempted to overlook this fundamental truth by the seemingly arbitrary nature of the investment process. According to Richard Charpie, managing general partner of Paine Webber Ventures, a major venture capital firm associated with Paine Webber, "We read 500 to 750 business plans a year—and we invest in six [6]. And the 500 to 750 that we read are only a fraction of those that are submitted." On this basis, obtaining investment funds seems a little like winning in a state lottery.

Assuming the worst, a frequent conclusion among potential entrepreneurs and others is: "We have less than one chance in a hundred to get money, so let's not knock ourselves out preparing a knockout of a business plan. They won't see us or talk to us without first seeing a business plan, so let's sling one together and get a foot in the door. After that, we'll convince them to make the investment we're looking for."

The usual result: no foot in the door, no interest in any

further discussions, and no investment. Worse yet, a second try with a better business plan is received with skepticism and built-in reservations.

The lesson: The business plan must be the best that can be written and packaged. The first shot is the most important. Therefore, the plan should read easily, it should be packaged appropriately, it should focus on the key issues, and it should do all the other things that make for an exciting document.

The business plan is truly the only real "foot in the door." It is the company's representative residing at the potential investor's premises. It speaks for the company, and it must speak appropriately and successfully.

In this introductory chapter, we consider the essential elements of a winning business plan, situations requiring business plans, the investor and lender perspectives, and the key criteria financiers use to begin evaluating plans.

Plans that Succeed

What does a winning business plan consist of? Based on our experience with the MIT Enterprise Forum, we have devised the following as the key requirements of a plan that will win funding:

• It must be arranged appropriately, with an executive summary, a table of contents, and its chapters in the right order.
• It must be the right length and have the right appearance—not too long and not too short, not too fancy and not too plain.
• It must give a sense of what the founders and the company expect to accomplish three to seven years into the future.
• It must explain in quantitative and qualitative terms the benefit to the user of the company's products or services.

- It must present hard evidence of the marketability of the products or services.
- It must justify financially the means chosen to sell the products or services.
- It must explain and justify the level of product development which has been achieved and describe in appropriate detail the manufacturing process and associated costs.
- It must portray the partners as a team of experienced managers with complementary business skills.
- It must suggest as high an overall "rating" as possible of the venture's product development and team sophistication.
- It must contain believable financial projections, with the key data explained and documented.
- It must show how investors can cash out in three to seven years, with appropriate capital appreciation.
- It must be presented to the most potentially receptive financiers possible to avoid wasting precious time as company funds dwindle.
- It must be easily and concisely explainable in a well-orchestrated oral presentation.

Situations Requiring Business Plans

We believe that every company needs a written business plan to guide its operations and ensure its viability and growth. The business that runs "by the seat of its pants" often winds up with torn pants. Day-to-day operations are subject to short-term ups and downs, and seemingly important side issues can consume resources and distract managers from their main line of activity and concentration.

A good business plan can keep a company's executives and key employees focused on major objectives. Most well-run corporations operate in accordance with a business plan that defines their goals and establishes the strategy and tactics for achieving objectives.

Thus, we believe managers should get into the habit of preparing business plans to cover a variety of business situations, as follows:

1. Startup ventures. New businesses seeking funding must almost always have a business plan, whether they are seeking equity or debt financing. We are also convinced that a written plan will help startups achieve excellence by charting the course to be followed by all parts of the business.

2. Existing companies seeking additional financing. Regardless of their size, companies requiring expansion capital should assemble a written plan to obtain funding at the most favorable rates. The plan also enables both managers and financiers to judge performance against the plan's projections.

3. New activities within existing companies. Recently a middle management executive of a large food manufacturer approached a member of the MIT Enterprise Forum's executive committee for assistance. He had conceived of a new product, and his group vice president had responded that, although the idea looked interesting, a full-blown business plan was needed to evaluate the product idea and decide on committing corporate funds. The executive committee member helped the manager write the plan, and the product development was authorized.

Clearly, corporate managers seeking to start new products or services or establish new divisions help their chances—and careers—if they have a convincing business plan. If the food company middle manager just discussed had handed his superior a complete business plan in the first place—instead of an orally described product idea—he would have been recognized immediately as a potential candidate for top management.

Designing and writing business plans that win backing is a skill that should be of vital interest to individuals in various aspects of business, as follows:

- Founders and executives of businesses of all sizes
- Ambitious employees, group leaders, and managers
- Business consultants, especially those who assist emerging companies
- Investors, bank executives, and other individuals who furnish funding, who can be better prepared to back promising businesses and monitor the progress of companies they finance

The Investor Perspective

No matter who is preparing the business plan, he or she must have an understanding and appreciation of how investors think and approach venture opportunities. Although we concentrate in this book on investors who back young businesses, corporate executives are also investors when they decide to fund new products, services, and divisions.

Perhaps the easiest way to understand the investor approach is to contrast it with the entrepreneur's usual approach. When it comes to investment, one of the most distinguishing traits of entrepreneurs is optimism. They see all the money to be made from their venture ideas and tend to downplay the risks.

This trait is extremely important and valuable because, without it, many businesses would never be started. It enables entrepreneurs to press ahead and exploit opportunities despite the skepticism of friends, relatives, employers, and others who may be wary of new ideas and who may focus instead on security. Entrepreneurs often have an important vision, and they refuse to let go of it despite endless obstacles.

Entrepreneurs may get used to the skepticism of friends and

relatives, but what often surprises—indeed, even shocks—
them are the reactions they frequently encounter when they
seek outside capital. If no one else appreciates the venture
idea or its initial success, they figure that professional investors and lenders should. After all, they're the pros. They
know good business ideas and can recognize legitimate opportunities.

In many cases, though, the professionals are not only skeptical but, at times, they may be more negative than all those
security-conscious friends and relatives. Why do they give the
cold shoulder?

Part of the disparity in attitudes is dictated by the simple
fact that, as we indicated previously, investors and lenders are
inundated with proposals. In their experience, there are many
more losers than winners. And even among the winners, there
are only a very few big winners—that is, companies which return 50% or more annually on investment, adjusted for inflation.

In addition, investors in emerging companies are constantly
weighing risk versus opportunity. Like investors since the beginning of time, they seek to maximize opportunity and minimize risk. Entrepreneurs may wonder how financial experts
involved with new and young ventures can be preoccupied
with risk. "That's something for corporate bankers and stock-
brokers to be concerned about," think the entrepreneurs.

Of course, venture investors know their investments aren't
as safe as blue-chips; therefore, the drive to reduce risks is
very strong. The aversion to risk helps explain why venture
capitalists will give previously successful entrepreneurs a full
hearing, occasionally even before they have a completed business plan. If they've succeeded once, the reasoning goes, the
chances of failure are reduced compared with inexperienced
entrepreneurs.

Investors must do more than minimize risk, though, if they are going to succeed. Investors in new and young ventures need to maximize returns from each of their holdings. Because the inherent risk in investing in young companies is greater than that for investing in established public companies, venture capital fund managers must promise investors in their firms larger overall returns than could be expected in money market funds, bonds, and stocks. To do that, fund managers must not only keep failures to a minimum, but they must have some big winners—companies with annual capital growth in the 50%-plus category—to offset the inevitable mediocre performers.

Lenders are investors in the sense that they extend financial backing in the hope that the business will grow, justifying ever-larger loans and other services that will net profits. But in contrast to professional investors, lenders are concerned mainly that their loans are repaid with interest. Thus, borrowers must succeed well enough to generate cash for debt service and loan repayment, usually over periods up to five years or more.

Some lenders and investors—insurance companies and small business investment companies (SBIC's), for instance—hedge their bets by making loans and negotiating options to invest at a later date at a pre-arranged price. These financiers then decide whether or not to actually invest, depending on how the company is performing. Such financial backing is typically referred to as a debt-equity combination.

A final trait of investors, in particular, that usually surprises entrepreneurs is the investors' relatively short attention span. Many entrepreneurs tend to see their ventures as lifetime commitments to success and growth and expect that anyone else who gets involved will have the same sense of timelessness. But when investors evaluate a business plan, they consider not only whether to get involved, but also how and when to get uninvolved.

Their time horizon has a simple explanation: Because small fast-growing companies have little cash available for dividends, the primary means for investors to profit is by selling their holdings. This often happens when the companies go public or are sold to large corporations. Venture capitalists are typically looking to liquidate small-company investments three to seven years down the road so as to pay gains to individual investors and generate funds for investment in new ventures. How to *cash out* with major capital appreciation is the chief concern of the professional investor.

The Entrepreneur as Investor

Aside from their goal of winning investment funds, founders must not lose sight of the fundamental fact that they, too, are investors. By virtue of starting and managing an enterprise, they are committing themselves to years of hard work and personal sacrifice. In the early years of a venture's life, they are likely giving up the higher earnings that would come from a regular job. And more often than not, entrepreneurs must throw in some or all of their personal savings to get the enterprise off the ground.

Therefore, it's essential that entrepreneurs be able to stand back and evaluate their own businesses objectively, in much the same way that professional investors evaluate businesses. That means assessing whether the opportunity for reward some years down the road truly justifies the risk early on.

How much of an up-front investment—in time, money, and energy—is required of the entrepreneur? How does the venture compare in terms of other opportunities the entrepreneur has? How long does the entrepreneur want to stay with the venture? How much will the venture likely be worth in three to seven years? The entrepreneur must consider those and other questions of the sort we will examine later in this chapter and in the remainder of this book.

When a young venture is viewed in such objective terms rather than through the rose-colored glasses through which entrepreneurs tend to view business opportunities, the final decision on whether or not to invest may change. That was the case with an entrepreneur who appeared at one of the first MIT Enterprise Forum sessions seeking financing for his young scientific instruments company.

In his mind, the venture had much long-term promise. But to panelists, the enterprise faced especially difficult marketing problems because its product was highly specialized and had, at best, an unusually small number of potential customers. That difficulty combined with the entrepreneur's already heavy debt load to get the venture started made the chances of eventual success quite slim. Moreover, because of his technical skills, he was in a position to command a sizable salary in a regular job.

The panelists concluded that the most optimistic outcome for the entrepreneur in pursuing this particular venture for another three to seven years was that he would have as much financial return as he would have had holding a job during that time. On the down side, he might wind up with much less financial return, in exchange for much larger headaches. After viewing the venture in such cool, dispassionate terms, the entrepreneur agreed with the panelists and gave it up.

Viewing enterprises from the investor's perspective means embracing the planning process, because only by going through an orderly and logical evaluation will the answers to the key questions regarding risk and return become clear.

Indeed, making the right decision is probably more important for the entrepreneur than for investors. Investors, after all, reduce their risk by investing in a portfolio of companies, a few of which are expected to perform poorly or fail. The entrepreneur puts all his or her eggs in one basket. If the enterprise doesn't work out, the investment game is over. And in the process, homes—even marriages—are sometimes lost.

Understanding Opportunity and Risk

Which basic traits in young ventures connote opportunity and risk in financiers' minds? We can begin to answer that question by examining in detail a case at the MIT Enterprise Forum and then considering it as well as other cases against themes that the venture capitalists, bankers, and financial consultants who serve as panelists repeatedly raise in their evaluations of enterprises.

Nancy C. appeared before the MIT Enterprise Forum not long ago on behalf of herself and her partner husband seeking $1.5 million of investment funds to enable their four-year-old computer software company to expand. At first glance, the company seemed to have much going for it.

Having started with just Nancy and her husband, the company, by the time of the presentation, had twenty-one employees and some big-name customers for its software. Moreover, the company was in a glamorous area of high technology— "bar-code data collection systems." Bar codes are the lines and numbers we commonly see on food packages which enable computerized cash registers to determine which specific items are being purchased and what their prices are.

Nancy's company had adapted the bar-code technology for use in factories, so that employees could easily record such information as the time they arrived, the items they were working on, how many pieces they'd assembled, and how long each task took. This makes valuable production data quickly available to managers so they can make production-line adjustments and spot bottlenecks before they become serious problems.

Only 1% of the industrial market for bar-code technology had yet been tapped and that market was expected to grow at a 20% to 60% annual pace, she said. Moreover, Nancy explained, her company had gotten into the market ahead of the "big boys"—Univac, Hewlett-Packard, "and even IBM."

"We have a superb leading edge of technology product and some very big name installations," she concluded. "We know where we want to go and we know where the marketplace is."

Sounds like the kind of situation investors should be throwing money at, right? Well, not exactly, as Nancy emotionally explained. "We are severely hampered by a lack of funds. We cannot move fast enough. Too much of our time is spent in the proverbial 'putting bread on the table.' We've been searching for venture capital for eight months now, with little success. I've been told by various people that we have a good business plan. I've been told that our growth has been phenomenal. I've been told that our client list is very impressive. . . ."

By considering certain of the basic criteria investors use to initially size ventures up, we quickly discover that Nancy's enterprise looked much different to professional investors—in both positive and negative respects—than it did to her. The investors' appraisal is explained in the next section.

Turning Investors On

As they skim through business plans, investors are looking for four ideal characteristics to pique their interest. This isn't to say that companies must possess all four of these characteristics to stand a chance of obtaining financing. It's just that having one or more grabs investors' attention and gets them to probe further.

The four turn-ons, in order of importance to investors, are as follows:

1. *Evidence of customer acceptance.* Investors like to know that the product or service a new venture will sell is being used, even if only on a trial or demonstration basis. Nancy C.'s company was in good shape on this score because it had gone beyond the trial or demonstrator phase and had actually sold several of its systems to bona fide customers. Moreover, the company had orders for additional systems on its books.

Investors have a few reasons for wanting to see a product or service being used. So much product specialization is occurring, in the high-technology area in particular, that it's nearly impossible to keep up with all the product possibilities. Besides, investors feel reassured if there is some indication that customers are receptive to a new company's product or service. They also feel reassured if they can go to a factory or store and actually view and touch a product or observe a service being used.

Finally, being able to view products and services in use enables financiers to talk to customers and learn their reactions. Getting such feedback often enables investors to judge with much greater certainty than otherwise whether a venture will exhibit 100% annual sales growth or just 20% growth—or perhaps nothing.

2. *Appreciation of investor needs.* Because investors usually want to cash their stock in somewhere between three and seven years after making their investment, they want to see some evidence that entrepreneurs have thought about how to

comply with this desire. Do the entrepreneurs expect to go public, sell the company, or buy the investors out in three to seven years? Will the proceeds provide investors with a return on invested capital commensurate with the investment risk— usually in the range of 35% to 60%, compounded and adjusted for inflation? In simple terms, the investor expects the amount invested to appreciate in value at the rate of 35% to 60% each year, compounded, and after allowing for inflation.

It was in this category that Nancy C.'s company began to fall considerably short of the mark in panelists' appraisals. The business plan made no statement of when or how investors might liquidate their holdings. And a panelist who did some arithmetic to calculate what the $1.5 million investment needed to be worth in five years to satisfy investor goals versus what the company looked likely to be worth concluded that the financiers "would need to own the entire company and then some." This simple evaluation—described in detail on pages 167 to 169—ruled out an investment of the size Nancy C.'s company was seeking.

3. *Evidence of focus.* Investors want a sense that founders know which one or two things their company does best and will concentrate its efforts on maximizing those strengths. Here, Nancy C.'s company also fell short. She noted with pride in her presentation and in the business plan that the company was marketing several software products in addition to the bar-code system; these products, though not directly related to the company's main product, helped provide badly needed income and had growth potential in their own right.

However, one Enterprise Forum panelist who advises small companies on strategies for obtaining financing saw nothing to be proud of. "If I were you, I would not mention in your final business plan the existence of these other products you have developed as a sideline. A venture capitalist reading your plan might well say, 'What are they doing with these other products? Aren't they taking away from the energy needed to market their main product?'"

Of the criteria investors use to do preliminary evaluation of developing ventures, this is probably the biggest surprise to entrepreneurs. They frequently feel as if they must demonstrate that all the company's eggs don't sit in one basket.

If one particular product or service doesn't sell as well as it should, there will be plenty of others around to make up for it and provide needed revenues, the rationale goes. Moreover, entrepreneurs feel that by pursuing a number of products or services, their companies will be in a position to reap tremendous profits if everything sells well.

Investors, however, know that companies that try to do too many things won't do any single thing well enough to allow for fast-track growth.

Take the case of perhaps the most diversified company ever to appear at the MIT Enterprise Forum. The company sold twenty-seven types of chemicals to realize annual sales of only $500,000. Under questioning by panel members, it turned out that one of the products accounted for 84% of sales. The panelists' advice was simple: Get rid of the twenty-six dogs and concentrate your energy on the one product bringing in most of the volume.

When entrepreneurs appear before investors with well-focused ventures, they are often on their way toward arousing significant interest. One entrepreneur at the MIT Enterprise Forum described a computer system his company had designed for gas stations to record credit purchases. Not only was the company focused on one significant product, but the product was focused on one significant market. That evidence of focus, together with some early indications of customer acceptance, helped the venture raise investment funds within a few weeks of its presentation.

4. *Proprietary position.* Exclusive rights to a product or process usually come in the form of patents; they may also be obtained via copyright or trademark protection. Had Nancy C. satisfied investor concerns about return on capital and focus, this trait would have contributed more positively to the company's image than it did, since her company had developed its own uniquely functioning software, giving it the protection of copyright laws. As one venture capitalist on the MIT Enterprise Forum panel evaluating the company observed, "The real profit potential may be in the license you have through your exclusive software."

Such protection is easier to obtain for products than for services. The most common way of gaining a proprietary position for a service is through registration of trademarks. Postal Instant Printing (PIP) and Weight Watchers are two service companies with well-known trademarks.

Financial backers of young ventures know that such government protection doesn't offer any guarantees of success. Indeed, patent, copyright, and trademark protection really only comprise tickets of admission to court to seek to prevent competitors from copying covered products and processes.

From an investor's perspective, though, a company in a proprietary position helps reduce risk because the practical effect of having legal protection is to limit competition. The classic case of a company benefiting from a proprietary position is Polaroid, which prospered for nearly thirty years before Kodak could devise an instant-printing process which didn't infringe on Polaroid patents.

In addition, a company in a proprietary position is likely to be a more attractive acquisition candidate three to seven years down the road, when investors seek to liquidate their holdings. Potential corporate acquirers, not surprisingly, are similarly interested in limiting competition.

Turning Investors Off

In the initial screening process, there are four danger signs that most stand out to financiers. Just as not having one of the turn-ons isn't a guarantee of rejection, raising a red flag also isn't cause for automatic rejection. But, of course, it is better to avoid them altogether than trouble investors with them.

The four turn-offs, in order of importance, are as follows:

1. *Product orientation.* If there is a single cause of excessive entrepreneur optimism, it is infatuation with the company's product or service rather than the market for the product or service. Focusing too heavily on the company's product or service, in investors' experience, usually comes at the expense of focusing on the wishes and needs of potential customers.

Two entrepreneurs who approached a member of the MIT Enterprise Forum executive committee for advice on starting a company had what at first glance seemed to be a winning product. They had devised an electronic calculator-type English language dictionary. Users could simply key in the first syllable of the word they wanted and scroll through words until the desired word came up. The device would also define words as well, after a "define" key was punched.

Unfortunately, the device would cost customers about $300. And it wouldn't really do anything that printed dictionaries, which cost $20 or less, can do. The executive committee member advised the entrepreneurs to drop the idea, at least until costs for the device declined considerably. But they were so enamored of the product that they pressed ahead, oblivious of a market which has yet to recognize their product.

Business plans which devote more space to describing the product than to detailing who will buy the product and how it will be sold make investors nervous that the company is really a playpen for the founders to fiddle with their latest gadgets.

2. *Projections which deviate excessively from industry norms.* In the electrical connector industry (plugs and sockets), an acceptable percent gross profit margin may be 30%, while in the medical instrumentation industry it is usually above 60%. (Percent gross profit margin is the sales receipts less the cost of goods sold divided by sales receipts multiplied by 100.)

If an electrical connector company forecast a 60% gross margin and a medical instrumentation company predicted a 30% margin, anyone familiar with the two industries would no doubt be skeptical of the results and wonder if either the connector company's projections were being inflated to the up side or if ineffective management was hampering the medical instrumentation company on the down side.

Each industry has its range of accepted financial results and marketing approaches. Entrepreneurs can determine likely profit margins, cost of sales, product prices, and so forth, by examining annual reports or 10K reports of public companies in their industry. If a fledgling company's business plan makes projections that are sharply at variance with what investors know are acceptable ranges in an industry, a red flag immediately goes up.

Thus, a company planning software based on very large scale integrated (VLSI) circuits came under criticism by an Enterprise Forum panelist on this point. Indeed, in this case, it wasn't as much a matter of deviating from an industry range as it was of deviating from all industries' ranges. "You show the highest gross margin of any company I have ever seen at the Enterprise Forum—93.6%," the panelist noted. "Either it has to be explained carefully or looked over for error. It raises a red flag to potential investors. Frankly, I don't think you could do this with mirrors."

Investors worry when they see projections which deviate from an industry norm because they suggest either that entrepreneurs haven't done their homework or they're being unduly optimistic.

3. *Unrealistic growth projections.* Not long ago, an entrepreneur appeared at an Enterprise Forum session for startup ventures and confidently described his company's new sixteen-bit portable computer. Looking four years down the road, he said with a straight face, he expected his company to be doing $400 million annual sales.

The panelists were barely able to contain their laughter. It wasn't as if they didn't believe a new venture could achieve such growth; companies like Compaq and Apple had already set enviable precedents. But, as several panelists politely explained to the entrepreneur, the home computer market had changed dramatically since Compaq and Apple achieved their remarkable growth. The market had matured and become more competitive, making it difficult for a newcomer to get space on retailers' shelves and establish a name in consumers' minds. Marketing had become much more important than technology. As a consequence, one panelist concluded that the business plan had "a dream-like quality."

As optimists, entrepreneurs tend to be unrealistic on the high side in their expectations of long-term growth. Investors know that and expect it. But when the projections begin losing touch with reality, all kinds of bells and whistles go off in investors' minds. Unless the spectacular projections are explained and argued quite convincingly in the business plan, investors are likely to conclude that the entrepreneur either hasn't done the necessary homework or is just unrealistic. Either deficiency doesn't do a lot to inspire confidence.

Only slightly less bothersome to investors are entrepreneurs who are unrealistic in their growth projections on the low side. At the same Enterprise Forum session at which the entrepreneur with the portable computer appeared, a woman leading a group of entrepreneurs from a software company made a pitch for several hundred thousand dollars. To her surprise, the panelists liked the product, created to help administrators design software to suit their own needs.

One panelist probably summed up the consensus when he advised, "You need to think bigger . . . You don't want to be undercapitalized if you're going to be a fast-growth company."

Unrealistic growth projections on the low side don't worry investors from a risk viewpoint. What concerns them is that the ventures won't reach their true potential because they'll be hampered by entrepreneurs who don't "think big" enough. Equally important, as we explain in the special section following Chapter 8, insufficient growth does not warrant venture capital investment.

4. *Custom or applications engineering.* When a company's basic product or service needs to be altered or specially designed for each customer, potential investors see high costs and low profits. For instance, Nancy C.'s software company needed to alter each of its computerized bar-code systems to take into account the vagaries of every customer's particular factory and assembly-line organization.

A member of the MIT Enterprise Forum panel expressed the problem to Nancy this way: "You are trying to increase sales significantly in your own market, but how can you achieve quantity if you do all this custom work? The profit is in the basic approach, not in all this custom engineering. What you might do is come up with two or three variations of your basic product which need relatively small amounts of customizing and could be sold almost on the job. Otherwise, you won't be able to hire staff people fast enough—the high-quality, high-tech people—and also train and pay them."

Consulting and architectural firms seeking to improve their growth rates tend to run into the same sort of problem. Because each client has a different need or project, the firms encounter difficulty in their efforts to expand quickly. Service businesses which find ways around the customizing obstacle by offering only a few variations of their basic offering—Federal Express and McDonald's are two examples—can achieve significant growth.

The problem posed by custom or applications engineering from investors' perspectives, then, is twofold. First, it increases selling costs, because specially trained personnel must be added to do the customized work. In some cases, costs are inflated, because companies which sell made-to-order products or services are forced into a bidding situation by government agencies or corporations, which want to pick and choose among various alternatives; the losing bidders, in particular, wind up expending much energy and money designing their products or services, often with nothing to show for their efforts. Even for the winners, it's difficult to show impressive profits in the face of such cost demands.

Second, individualized production reduces the opportunity for achieving economies of scale. Specially designed products or alterations can't be mass-produced like nuts and bolts or cars. Once a mass-produced item reaches a certain quantity level, production costs per unit decline dramatically, allowing profits to rise quickly.

All this isn't to say that companies that rely on specially designed products or services can't be successful. But from the viewpoint of trying to raise investor funds, entrepreneurs forming such companies should expect resistance. Investors usually don't see the promise of exceptional sales and profit growth in enterprises that have unusual custom sales costs. And with so many ventures to choose from, investors tend to simply reject such opportunities unless the products can be clearly proven to provide exceptional cash flow and profits.

Conflicting Pressures

Part of the challenge for entrepreneurs as they assemble business plans, then, is to convince investors that the new venture will exploit high-growth opportunities while minimizing possible risks. That means entrepreneurs must adjust their strategies to accentuate their companies' strengths and anticipate concerns about weaknesses. If a business has a proprietary product which requires custom engineering, thorough consideration must be given to maximizing the advantage conferred by being proprietary and minimizing—or justifying—the amount of custom work necessary.

Entrepreneurs in that situation can't hope to impress investors by merely playing up the proprietary aspects and ignoring the custom requirements. Both positives and negatives must be confronted head-on and discussed explicitly in the business plan so that possible red flags become less threatening in investors' minds. Much of this book is devoted to understanding and handling the dual pressures of venture strengths and weaknesses.

Another part of the challenge for entrepreneurs is recognizing that the assembling of the business plan is more than simply a writing assignment. It's a process of building a business and effectively articulating where the business has been, where it is now, and where it is headed. The business plan, then, embodies the business and sells it.

In the process of preparing the business plan, the management team develops clear perceptions of its objectives, obligations, and opportunities. We recommend strongly that all managements go through this highly self-educational process.

The next chapter specifies the most effective ways of packaging the business plan so that it becomes the best business embodiment and selling document possible.

IN SUMMARY

Business plans have become an essential fact of life for companies at all stages of development. To succeed, plans must clearly and concisely convey the state of the venture and its future objectives. In approaching the planning process, entrepreneurs should seek to understand the investor perspective in evaluating ventures and view themselves as investors of time and money.

In initially assessing business plans, investors are turned on by the following:

• Evidence of customer acceptance of the venture's product or service

• An appreciation of investors' needs, through recognition of their particular financial return goals

• Evidence of focus, through concentration on only a limited number of products or services

• Proprietary position, as expressed in the form of patents, copyrights, and trademarks

Investors tend to be turned off by the following:

• Infatuation with the product or service rather than familiarity with and awareness of marketplace needs
• Financial projections at odds with accepted industry ranges
• Growth projections out of touch with reality
• Custom or applications engineering, which make substantial growth difficult

2

Judging a Book by Its Cover

THE SCENE: The offices of the Go For Broke Venture Capital Company

THE SETTING: The weekly meeting of its partners, Messrs. A. and B., Ms. C. and Ms. D., led by chairman E.

E: Let's start with John A. and get his report on "Super Software, Inc."

A: They sent me a sloppy and faded collection of photocopied sheets, with no cover, summary, page numbers, or table of contents. It didn't even have a return address or a title, not to mention a date. If they treat their own important property this badly, we could probably kiss our money goodbye.

E: Any other friendly comments?

A: Yeah—I couldn't figure out what they were trying to sell until I got through all the typos and misspellings to page 50—and by then I had lost interest. Looks like a pretty disorganized bunch of people. I also couldn't figure out what they're looking for from investors, so I guess they can't either.

E: Let's pass up Super Software—on to the next. Frank B., what did you think of that Same Day Package Service?

B: I was pleasantly surprised. It's well presented—bound in a nice, simple blue plastic cover and it's well organized and easy to read. It has a great one-page summary, which reads so well I would be happy to read it to all of you. Then you would get an immediate idea of what the company is, what it's looking for, and where it's headed. After that, there's an excellent table of contents. The business plan itself is forty pages long and organized nicely into readable sections. I couldn't find a single typo—and you all know how tough I am on poorly presented plans. This Same Day Package bunch evidently is well organized. I recommend we invite them in to make a presentation next Tuesday.

E: Okay—bring 'em in. They sound like potential winners. I sometimes wonder whether the groups of people who ask us for financing realize that we are just as much interested in finding good companies to invest in as the companies are in finding people to invest in them. Linda C., would you like to report on that graphics company you were grappling with?

C: Frankly, I couldn't get through the damn plan. It's about as long as the Manhattan phone book and not nearly as interesting. What with my other assignments, I don't think I'll finish reading it for three months. I'm certain it could easily be reduced to less than one-fourth its present size, though, with some of the detail incorporated into a second volume which we could refer to once we decided we had some interest in the project.

E: Okay, so it's long and tedious. From what you were able to read, does it look like an interesting company?

C: It's almost impossible to tell. It has to do with a technology we're interested in, but they don't get to the point, and I'm still not sure what they're trying to sell or to whom. Most long and wordy business plans like this one are trying to cover a lack of direction and poor internal organization. Massive verbiage makes me suspicious.

E: Okay—send it back to them. Mary D., what about the Marvelous Machine Company and the extra fancy business plan?

D: What an astonishing publishing job! It's hardcover bound, like the old library books used to be, and the pages themselves are works of art. The plan itself isn't bad—we probably should look into the company—but I'm suspicious that they'll take our money, build themselves super-beautiful offices, buy Ferraris for all of the officers, and simply spend too much on form rather than on content. I was interested enough to visit our printer and check the cost of a book like this one. I was told that the printing and binding alone was worth more than $150 per copy in the small quantities in which business plans are printed. Frankly, I'm turned off.

E: When will they learn how to present their business plans in such a way as to grab our attention—and investment?

This dialogue is an imaginary but accurate representation of the frustration, skepticism, and occasional satisfaction financiers feel when they examine business plans. Given the competition for investors' and lenders' attention, business plans must be easy to read and comprehend. This chapter, then, advises on three aspects of the plan's presentation:

1. How the business plan should look
2. How it should be organized
3. How it should be assembled

Creating Favorable Initial Impressions

Panelists at the MIT Enterprise Forum usually begin their commentaries with some observations about the business plan's appearance. After all, it creates the first impression to financiers about the company and its principals.

What do the panelists expect? In general, they want the plan to look good, but not too good. They want it to be the right length. They want a short, precise, and clear explanation early on that demonstrates a complete understanding by the principals of all aspects of the business of the company. They don't want to be offended with bad grammar, many typos, or inexcusable spelling errors.

Investors are looking for evidence that the principals treat their own property with care—and will likewise treat the investment carefully. In other words, form is just as important as content, and the panelists know that good form reflects good content, and vice versa. Most of the time we *can* judge a book by its cover.

To create a favorable first impression, business plans must have the following:

The right appearance. A plastic spiral binding, holding together a pair of cover sheets of a single color, provides both a neat appearance and sufficient strength to withstand being handled by a number of people without damage. As was demonstrated in the hypothetical meeting of the venture capital firm's partners at the start of this chapter, the binding and printing must not appear either too sloppy or too rich.

A stapled compilation of photocopied pages will usually not be treated seriously, and book-type binding with typeset pages will arouse suspicions. At one MIT Enterprise Forum session, a panelist took the presenting entrepreneurs to task for presenting a business plan he felt to be too fancy. "I am quite uncomfortable with the fact that it is typeset, and I think most venture capitalists would be put off by a typeset document," he said. "It doesn't come across as a custom document assembled for targeted investors. Neat typewriter work or word processing work is all that is required. If you get fancier than that, investors are likely to get the feeling that you are covering something up."

How long should the plan be? We strongly believe that a business plan should be approximately forty pages in length. In fact, it should be possible to outline both the business and the plans of nearly any enterprise, even the Chevrolet division of General Motors, within forty pages. Although the first draft of a business plan may greatly exceed our recommended length, editing must produce a final version that fits within the forty-page ideal.

This brings to mind the story about Voltaire, the great French writer and philosopher, who wrote novels commissioned by noblewomen. He sent one commissioned novel to a patroness with the note "Madam, enclosed please find the novel that you commissioned. I have written it in two volumes. If I had more time, I could have written it in one." The lesson here is condense, condense, condense.

It is often useful to generate an additional volume to the business plan, containing the detailed supporting information that will be helpful to the investor during the investigative, or "due diligence," period that will occur if there is initial interest. All that we have said about business plans of ideal length does not apply to the backup information made available to support the statements made in the business plan proper.

In a psychological sense, the "due diligence" volume provides a relief valve for those people in the company who can't resist including all sorts of detailed information in the description of the company and its business. The details serve a useful function in volume two, provided that they are relevant and truly support the contentions of the business plan.

The cover and title page. It may seem obvious, but it is important to emphasize that the cover should bear the name of the company, its address and phone number, and the month and year in which the plan is issued. Surprisingly, a large number of business plans are submitted to potential investors without a return address or a phone number to easily enable an intrigued investor to contact the company and request further information or express an interest, either in the company or in some aspect of the plan.

At an MIT Enterprise Forum session, a panelist noted that the absence of the company address and telephone number on the business plan he had reviewed had cost him nearly half an hour looking through telephone books and calling directory assistance to track the company down for further information. "It drives me crazy," he sighed as he admonished the entrepreneurs on this seemingly trivial but nonetheless important point.

Inside the front cover should be a well-designed title page, which once again gives the name of the company, its address, and its telephone number. Very often, the chief executive officer is listed, because the first contacts will likely be made with this person. Again, the month and year are listed so that those receiving the plan will know that it is recent and represents the most up-to-date thinking of the company.

In an upper or lower corner should be the legend, "Copy Number ———." Lawyers know that only a limited number of business plans should be circulated and that it is wise to make a record of the number of plans issued and the places to which they have been sent.

There is also a psychological advantage to holding down the number of copies outstanding—usually to no more than

twenty. No investor likes to think that the prospective investment is shopworn. (This is one of the situations in which a low
serial number proclaims a better product—as in etchings or
lithographs.)

A venture capitalist speaking at a recent seminar on financing
put it this way: "The first thing I look for is the copy number on
the plan. If it's over 20, I don't look much further."

The executive summary. The two pages immediately following
the title page should be the executive summary. Unbeknownst
to many entrepreneurs, this is the most important single part
of the business plan.

These two pages must crisply and concisely explain the following:

1. The company's current status
2. The products or services the company will sell and to
whom it will sell them
3. The benefits, in economic and non-economic terms, that
the company's products or services will confer on customers
4. The financial forecasts
5. The company's overall objectives three to seven years
into the future and how it proposes to reach those objectives
6. How much money the business requires to achieve its
objectives
7. How and when the investor is likely to benefit from the
investment

If all this seems like a tall order for a two-page summary,
that's because it is. But it can be done, and it *should* be done.
The two-page executive summary is what will sell the venture
capitalist or other investor on the wisdom of reading the rest
of the plan—or forgetting the whole thing.

The two or three minutes required to read the executive

summary are perhaps the most important few minutes in the entire life of many companies. In these few minutes, a key investor may become fascinated enough to read further or may become confused or turned off enough to move on to the next plan.

The table of contents. After the executive summary, there must be a well-designed table of contents. Each of the business plan's sections should be listed and the pages for each section clearly marked.

We feel that section or chapter numbering is superior to simple sequential page numbering. For example, the section entitled "The Market and Marketing Strategy" might be Section 2 in some business plans. In that case, the actual pages would be identified as from 2-1 to 2-11 in the table of contents, thus identifying each page within the section as belonging to that specific section. Likewise, each page of the marketing and sales section would be numbered 4-1 to 4-7. (Surprisingly, many business plans fail to contain numbered pages.) Any tables or figures should also bear page numbers that relate to the section in which they are found. The same approach should be employed in all sections of the business plan.

The sections that make up the business plan usually have important subsections within them. For example, the first section, which usually describes "THE COMPANY," may have such subsections as "Current Status" and "Management." It is useful and customary to include these subsections in the table of contents. This allows the prospective investor to quickly find any subject that may be of interest or importance without loss of time—or temper.

The sample table of contents on pages 32-33 illustrates both the structure and content of a business plan that most venture capital investors would find attractive.

Sample Table of Contents

Note: Additional separate entries for tables and figures should be provided using the same page-numbering method, e.g.: Product Data, Table 1, Page 3-5, etc.

Structure and Content

Various consultants in recent years have put together master business plans that can be adapted to any venture simply by filling in certain particulars at various points in the master plan. The approach isn't unlike that taken by lawyers in putting together standard wills and contracts.

Sophisticated investors disagree strongly with such "cookie-cutter" approaches to writing business plans, simply because the financiers believe that each business is unique, with its own special marketing, sales, production, and other issues. The investors may not be able to spot a cookie-cutter plan as such, but they will recognize deficiencies in the plan—perhaps devoting excessive or insufficient attention to various subjects, according to the layout of the master plan.

Nevertheless, we feel that sections of the business plan should adhere to certain guidelines proven attractive to investors in terms of structure and content, according to the preceding table of contents, as follows:

1. *The company.* Initially, entrepreneurs should describe the company—its origins, its expectations, and the management team. This section should summarize the enterprise's overall objectives so that the investor gets a clear indication early on of where the company is going and how it plans to get there.

2. *The market.* Within the business plan, as we have noted, the definition of the market to be served by the company is second in importance only to the definition of the company itself. An important part of that market definition is a description of the benefits to the user of the company's products or services. Investors want evidence that founders have a clear idea of who will purchase the company's product or service and why. That is, entrepreneurs must demonstrate that they focus primarily on the market their company will serve rather than on the technicalities of their product or service.

3. *Products (or services).* This third section describes the company's products or services, including a summarized theory of operation and a statement about performance and present status. The proprietary, patented, or patentable features of the company's products should also be summarized in this section. We recommend that the section on the company's products or services be a page or two shorter than the section on the company's market, as an indication to potential investors that the

founders realize the priority of markets over products. Investors are interested in companies which are market-driven, not product-driven.

4. *Sales*. After reading descriptions of the markets in Section 2 and the products in Section 3, investors will want to know precisely how the company plans to approach its customer prospects and thus capitalize on its potential. In this section, the business plan should state just how the goods or services are to be sold—whether by sales representatives, distributors, in-house salespeople, direct mail, or executive selling. Whichever approach is chosen, it must be clearly outlined and logically justified. This section should also discuss and justify sales costs and compare them with industry practices. The reader must come away with the conviction that the marketing plan will be implemented successfully via the sales approach.

5. *Manufacturing*. This section should cover the company's make/buy decisions. These can be justified by summarized supporting information. Investors want to see the manufacturing process being as inexpensive and efficient as possible, geared to maximizing profits. In preparing the business plan, an emphasis on value engineering (designs to minimize costs) will be viewed favorably. Also, entrepreneurs should include plans for quality control, since the investors will want to be aware of expected warranty costs associated with the product—and how they will be kept to a minimum.

Any discussion on development should be quite brief since, ideally, product or service development will be well along. Investors want their money to go into manufacturing and selling rather than into developing a product that is not yet ready to be sold. Consequently, inordinate development expenses and procedures will likely turn off most investors. Engineering in support of manufacturing, on the other hand, is well understood because it should be translated into better products and increased profits.

6. *Financial data.* This section should summarize previous financial performance, if any. Financial projections are customary in this section and should be realistic and justifiable so that the prospective investor does not feel that the numbers come out of *Alice in Wonderland.* To this end, those in the company who make up the financial data section are well advised to study the annual reports and the 10K reports filed by other companies in the same field. In the "due diligence" process, investors will check out industry practice and will avoid those companies which deviate too markedly from the successful customs of others in the same field. Finally, the financial data should be concise, avoiding the increasingly popular practice of including page after page of computer-generated spreadsheets. Investors are turned off by such programmed presentations, suspecting that such excessive data can conceal inappropriate financial planning.

7. *The investment.* This last formal section in the business plan should cover the entrepreneurs' expectations about the investment itself. This section should indicate how much money the company is seeking to raise, the form of investment being sought, how the funds will be used, and what portion of the company the investment will purchase. The description of the investment offering should include some discussion of the method whereby the company will provide the investor both an appropriate multiple of the investment and liquidity within a reasonable length of time—usually five years or less.

8. *Appendix.* This should be confined to résumés of the management team and key personnel. It might also include expla-

nations of financial or other data, but in any case it shouldn't extend the business plan beyond the ideal of forty pages. As we mentioned previously, detailed elaboration of any sections should appear in a second volume.

We recommend that this same format be followed by entrepreneurs seeking investment or loan funds. In addition, this approach is appropriate for corporate managers proposing a new project or charting the course a division or company expects to follow in upcoming years.

Companies which place a premium on long-term planning devote considerable effort to revising their business plans on an annual basis, to adjust for changes within the company and in the marketing environment. One corporation we know of practically shuts down for a week each year as its managers revise the company's business plan.

Writing and Editing

This is the task that most intimidates many entrepreneurs. If they don't feel comfortable or confident about their writing and editing in general, then the business-plan preparation process will only exacerbate their feelings of insecurity. After all, the business plan is probably the most difficult writing-editing project there is.

There's no need for entrepreneurs to go through this entire process alone, though. Many independent writers, consultants, and major accounting firms can assist in the preparation of business plans. Indeed, some consulting and accounting firms have set up departments specializing in business-plan preparation.

Those entrepreneurs who seek outside assistance to help in the writing and editing should realize that it's extremely important that *they* furnish the business information to be included in the plan. If the basic starting information is complete and logical, the business plan itself can be made into a winning document. However, to borrow an expression from the computer field—"garbage in, garbage out." (We discuss further the use of outsiders in aiding the business-plan process in Chapter 9.)

Thus, we feel that the business executives themselves are the appropriate authors of at least the first draft of the business plan. This approach allows the plan to be an expression of their own viewpoints and vision of the future of their company.

Each executive in the company's management team should prepare the chapter or chapters appropriate to her or his responsibility and expertise. This will lead to a composite document in which there will likely be great disparities in writing style. However, this document can then be edited and shaped into a coherent and cohesive plan that will accurately represent the company—and not present some idealized (and incorrect) picture constructed by an outside writer.

If all versions of the business plan are prepared by outsiders and "prettied up" in the process, contradictions may develop between what the company really can do and what the writer projects or predicts. These contradictions will likely become apparent to investors during the "due diligence" process. Consequently, it really is best that the company itself prepare a full-scale first draft.

Preparing the first draft of a business plan will likely be the most grueling writing assignment that the company's founders will ever tackle. When the sections are passed around to other members of the management team, tempers may flare and emotions run high; the conflicts that arise may need some smoothing over by the chief executive.

Despite the tension that may result, we recommend that all sections of the business plan be read, edited, and criticized by all members of the management team in preparation for assembly into a single document. The completed first draft may very well resemble a camel (a horse designed by a committee), but differences in writing styles and format can be resolved by good editing and a sense of humor.

The first draft of the business plan should be reviewed by the company's lawyer and patent counsel (where appropriate). The lawyer will eliminate excessively positive statements and substitute tentative ones.

For example, some business plans submitted to the MIT Enterprise Forum proclaim unequivocally that the investor will receive a return of at least 50% annually on the investment. Review by competent legal counsel would have forbidden the use of such definite language in forecasting return on investment. The Enterprise Forum suggests that the plan be reviewed before presentation—or risk lawsuits or adverse action by the SEC and, possibly, a few years in a quiet place with bars on the windows.

The legal counsel selected should have experience in dealing with investors, bankers, the Securities and Exchange Commission, and investments in general. It may also be necessary to submit the plan to patent counsel so that it avoids statements which would prejudice the company's position with regard to either domestic or foreign patents, licenses, and so on. Or it may be that the patent counsel can provide a letter which can be included in the appendix stating that the company's patent applications are likely to be accepted. This can be extremely useful in impressing investors.

Entrepreneurs are also well advised to show their first draft to an accounting firm or to a financial adviser who has experience in dealing with investments and investor-investee negotiations. The adviser should review projected financial figures, return on investment estimates, and financial statement formats, making sure that standard form is adhered to. In their efforts to produce a business plan that is in every way investor friendly, entrepreneurs must make an effort to present the financials in the form least likely to produce aggravation, questions, or suspicion.

Panelists at the MIT Enterprise Forum frequently complain about business plans that include reams of VisiCalc or other spreadsheet data in the business plan. The company's product may be novel—but the financials presented had better be in a standard form, or they won't be accepted.

After the first draft of the business plan has been written and reviewed by the various executives and outside professional advisers, it must be molded into a readable document that prospective investors will find attractive. At this point, the executives will probably do well to submit the plan to professional editors or writers for review of such things as grammar, syntax, consistency, clarity, and organization.

One of the best business plans ever submitted to the MIT Enterprise Forum had been edited by a faculty member of a major university business school who had a background in English literature. Free-lance writers who specialize in business journalism or regional editors of trade magazines may be useful in editing the business plan. Such writers and editors are accustomed to expressing their ideas in a way that will keep their audience's interest.

Another editing source—though more of the critique variety—can be members of venture capital firms who are friendly with any of the principals but whose venture capital companies will not be approached for investment funds. Such individuals can contribute very useful editorial ideas and quite often will be able to say, "Beef up Section 3," or, "Remove some of the jargon in Section 5 that will be understood only by highly trained readers. Consider the investor to be a member of the general public, and make sure that the prerequisite to reading your business plan is not a Ph.D. in your product area."

One of the best business plans ever submitted to the MIT Enterprise Forum had been reviewed by the following: *(a)* two venture capital partners whose firms were not going to be approached by the company; *(b)* a librarian with a remarkable gift for simplifying language; and, *(c)* a professional outside editor. The plan impressed the panelists immensely and ultimately received serious consideration by five venture capital companies of the eight to which it was submitted. The company raised over $4 million.

Professional writers and editors know well that the secret to successful writing is frequent rewriting. Therefore, our message is edit, edit, edit.

And before any business plan is sent out to investors, it should be carefully proofread. Misspellings and typos, as we've warned repeatedly, carry a strong negative message to financiers.

The Most Ideal Form

Of all the hundreds of business plans that have been submitted to the MIT Enterprise Forum, one stands out as so exemplary in its format that it can serve as a model plan. This plan was like other plans in that it contained text on each right-hand sheet through the book; what distinguished it from other plans was that each page was summarized on the left-hand page. That is, each left-hand page—left blank in other plans—contained sets of bulleted highlight phrases, so that it was possible to read the summarized version of the entire business plan in somewhat under ten minutes!

Those of us who reviewed the plan and appeared as panelists when the company made its presentation to the MIT Enterprise Forum all felt that we had seen the ultimate in business plans. Each of us approached it the same way: We read the summary through, from cover to cover, to gain an overview of the company's objectives and approaches to achieving them. Once our appetites were sufficiently whetted, we then read the detailed document. This business plan truly turned into a book we couldn't put down until we had read through to the last page—in one sitting!

IN SUMMARY

Business plans must convey in their appearance a sense of professionalism, clarity, and completeness. Toward that end, they should incorporate the following features:

- A plastic spiral binding
- A length not to exceed forty pages
- A cover and title page with company name, address, and copy number
- A two-page executive summary which captures the company's current status and future direction
- A table of contents and numbered pages
- Content that is at once original and that also follows guidelines professional financiers are known to prefer
- Professional editing to assess such presentation issues as grammar, clarity, and organization
- Appropriate legal disclaimers and financial forecasts, based on review by experienced lawyers and accountants

---

3

What Do You Want to Be When You Grow Up?

Children usually take a simplistic approach to the question which is this chapter's title, talking in terms of being a fireman, a race car driver, or a baseball player. By the time high school and college roll around, of course, the question becomes infinitely more complex. It isn't necessarily answered once we make a career choice, though. Investors will want to know how entrepreneurs answer the question, both on behalf of themselves and on behalf of their ventures.

For entrepreneurs, the above question is often one of the most difficult ones they must deal with, simply because the answer must satisfy their objectives, satisfy investors' objectives, and be realistically achievable. The answer forms the basis of the business plan, enabling entrepreneurs to begin dealing with marketing, financial, and other managerial issues.

Entrepreneurs must supply their answer in Section 1 of the business plan, "The Company," as part of a description of near-term, long-term, and management objectives. (See the sample table of contents, pages 32–33.) This chapter is devoted, first, to explaining how individuals starting and expanding businesses should assess their personal and company options so as to come up with a coherent and sensible state-

ment of management objectives. The chapter then examines
how management objectives should be analyzed in terms of
industry realities and investor goals to arrive at realistic near-
term and long-term company objectives.

A case that came before the MIT Enterprise Forum not
long ago perhaps best illustrates the dilemma the question
often poses.

Two entrepreneurs described their plan to start a large-scale
consulting firm which would assemble and sell proprietary
marketing information from data bases they would establish
on specific industries, such as personal computers or health-
care. Such data bases could then be sold in the form of floppy
disks at high prices to many companies needing such information, the entrepreneurs reasoned.

"Market research is really perking up," explained one of
the entrepreneurs, Harold B. "In this business, you've got to
find the unique thing. Our thing is the industry orientation . . . Our objective is to establish a series of data bases
much along the lines of the Dow Jones newswire and data
retrieval service. It will eventually be self-fulfilling in that it
will be automated and there will be a product manager running each industry-specific data base."

He projected that the company would have $3 million to $5
million revenues within two years and in the vicinity of $10
million in five years, with a pre-tax profit margin "pushing
40%." "In order to get there, however, we need a large
amount of money up-front to support a major effort in market
research, data gathering, and establishment of the data bases
that would later be sold to customers."

The Enterprise Forum panelists were especially concerned
about the founders' goals for themselves and their business.
One panelist noted that both entrepreneurs had previously
worked for a slow-growing consulting firm and wondered why,

from a personal viewpoint, they suddenly wanted to start a fast-growing business. He expressed concern that neither had any experience guiding a fast-growing business.

The panelist also pointed out that consulting firms tend to be smaller businesses—one- and two-person firms. What made these entrepreneurs think they could be different and start a fast-growth consulting business?

Said another panelist: "You are a people-oriented business and that is a really important asset. But every time the elevators go downstairs at 5 p.m., the company's entire assets are on them. How would you overcome that worry in the investors' minds?"

And a third panelist said in concluding the session: "I don't think this company should go for venture capital. My reasoning is that while these gentlemen are obviously very good at what they do, they are not comfortable with the sort of projections and presentations venture capitalists demand . . . This business can be bootstrapped and probably should be."

Clearly, the panelists in the role of potential investors were having trouble understanding the venture and its goals. In large part, that was because the business plan did not make a convincing case by explaining what the entrepreneurs and the business expected to be when they grew up.

Such cases are fairly common. Some entrepreneurs come to the MIT Enterprise Forum with ideas for promising companies and they expect to raise venture capital financing. But the ideas aren't right for the venture capitalists.

Somehow the question of how the companies will develop and what they will achieve hasn't been answered in a way that satisfies venture capital investment criteria. Or the question has been dealt with and the answer isn't what the venture capitalists are looking for.

Not only must founders have objectives for themselves and

for their companies, but these goals must be appropriate to the companies' industries and must mesh with the objectives of potential investors and lenders who are approached. And the fact that these issues have been thought out and resolved must come through clearly in the business plan. Otherwise, entrepreneurs can expect to waste much time and energy trying to sell what may be a perfectly fine business idea to financiers who admire the idea but aren't likely backers.

Delineating and matching the objectives of all concerned is no easy task, simply because there are so many options and possibilities. Essentially, entrepreneurs must seek to address four basic issues before they can come to an intelligent answer for the overriding question, what do you want to be when you grow up? They are as follows:

1. What do the founders want for themselves?
2. What do the founders want for their company?
3. How well do the founder and company objectives fit with the experiences of other businesses in the venture's industry?
4. What are the investors' or lenders' objectives?

The remainder of this chapter will consider these issues and offer advice for meshing these varying, and often conflicting, objectives.

The Founders' Objectives

At first glance, all founders would seem to have pretty much the same objective: to start a successful company that makes them rich. But in probing further, the issue of founder objectives isn't such a simple one to resolve because it involves both personal and business aspects. Some individuals want to start a business in the hope that a few years down the line it will be doing well enough financially that they can take long vacations. Others want the challenge of managing a fast-growing enterprise, with its constantly changing people, production, and marketing problems. And some want something in between.

What follows is a typology we have developed to help entrepreneurs determine their own objectives. Founders aren't expected to include statements of their individual objectives in the text of the business plan; rather, this typology can be used, together with the section that follows on the venture's objectives, to draft a convincing statement in Section 1 of the business plan on the management's overall objectives.

Entrepreneurs should also be prepared to explain their business and personal objectives to potential investors during the presentation and negotiation process. Panelists frequently ask founders at MIT Enterprise Forum sessions, "What do you want for yourself out of this venture?"

The president of a young specialty service business answered by saying, "I want to guide the company to $15 million sales after three years, at which time I expect to bring in seasoned professional managers who know more about managing maturing growth companies than I do. I'll gradually ease myself out of the business and go on to something else." The panelists were clearly impressed that the entrepreneur could so clearly and realistically articulate his own goals.

Taking business and personal needs together, entrepreneurs will likely discover that their objectives fall into one or several of the following categories:

Starting pitcher. This is the inveterate entrepreneur, the person who thrives on the venture creation process. The starting pitcher gets his or her team through the first five innings or so and then turns the game over to the relief pitchers. In the business startup game, of course, those first few innings determine ultimate survival.

The starting pitcher in new ventures loves to put the pieces of the new business together—making the prototype product, assembling a management team, obtaining financing, and wooing the potential customers. Once the business is all together and working the way it was intended, the starting pitcher begins to lose interest. As one starting pitcher we know puts it, "Once the important issues become a matter of exactly which health insurance or pension plan to offer, then I know it's time for me to move on."

What the starting pitcher most wants to move on to, not surprisingly, is another new venture. And the most common way of doing that is to sell his or her interest in the company and use the proceeds to start the next business.

Professional entrepreneur. This individual wants to start a fast-growing business and stay with it through his or her life and the company's life. That means going through all the company's stages—from the startup and survival stages to the stage when the company becomes profitable. If the entrepreneur is fortunate, it may also mean continuing growth that carries the company on through going public and toward Fortune 1000 status.

The classic case of the professional entrepreneur is Kenneth Olsen, founder of Digital Equipment Corporation, the Maynard, Mass., computer company. He was one of the founding partners in the 1950s and recalls vividly the time he spent during the earliest days cleaning the plant, designing the original minicomputer product, and obtaining venture capital.

He has guided the company through an amazing growth path and is today head of a multibillion-dollar giant that is a member of the Fortune 500. It's a difficult feat to carry out successfully, if only because going through so many stages requires an array of management skills that few entrepreneurs possess (or care to acquire).

Have-your-cake-and-eat-it-too entrepreneur. This individual is kind of a cross between the starting pitcher and the professional entrepreneur. Like the starting pitcher, this entrepreneur starts a company with the idea of selling it five to ten years down the road for a capital gain. But like the professional entrepreneur, once this individual gets the cake, or in this case the cash, he or she wants to eat it, too, by staying on and guiding the company under some other company's ownership.

The have-your-cake entrepreneur thus wants both the financial rewards of starting and selling a successful company and the professional-ego rewards of continuing to guide the company through future stages of growth. The hard part of the equation for many entrepreneurs is really eating the cake. Once they sell their companies, many entrepreneurs find that running the business for someone else just isn't as much fun as running the company for themselves. Similarly, sharing authority with an outsider isn't something many entrepreneurs take to very well. Studies have shown that fewer than half of acquired managements stay with their companies more than three years. Only in those cases in which the acquiring company truly leaves the original management team alone can the arrangement work well.

The inventor-researcher entrepreneur. This person views the fledgling business as a kind of laboratory for concocting new products, processes, or services. Computer engineers, biochemists, and other specialized professionals who become frustrated with their work in large corporations or as consultants often decide that the best way to achieve the freedom—and wealth—they're looking for to pursue their own projects is simply to start their own companies.

Many of these entrepreneurs wind up at the MIT Enterprise Forum, often as teams of three of four officers of a new company. These entrepreneurs both tantalize and frustrate the panelists, who see the promise of their innovative projects and the obstacles to the founders becoming effective managers.

Such entrepreneurs seem to have the best chances of succeeding when they recognize their managerial weaknesses and have the good sense to bring in experienced executives to run the financial and marketing sides of the enterprise. It's when they fancy themselves as well-rounded chief executives that these individuals sometimes get themselves and their businesses into trouble.

The lifestyle entrepreneur. This individual mainly wants the business to provide as nice a living as possible. Essentially, the business becomes an annuity that enables the entrepreneur to take exotic vacations, buy second and third homes, perhaps a yacht, and in general enjoy the good life.

This entrepreneur doesn't want the business to show extraordinary growth or to get too big, because growth and bigness mean problems. He or she doesn't want to have to worry about obtaining additional financing or hiring managers who ask to negotiate equity kickers.

One lifestyle entrepreneur we know produces specialty clothing for other companies. He arranges for subcontractors to do the actual production rather than owning any of his own plants. He has a core of steady wholesale customers who regularly purchase his goods. The business does about $2.5 million annual sales, of which our lifestyle entrepreneur realizes between $300,000 and $500,000. He has a house in Switzerland, where he takes long vacations.

This entrepreneur has a different outlook on his life and his business than do the other entrepreneurs we have described. Just as there's really no business to sell (without the owner) for a possible capital gain, there's also little in the way of potential liability or loss should he decide to exit the business, since he owns no plants or inventory. There's just lots of cash as long as the owner wants to stick with the venture.

The Venture's Objectives

In the course of writing the business plan the founders of a new company should come to a decision for transforming their individual objectives into a single company objective. That objective is really a function of the alternatives possible for new companies as they become established and grow.

Among possible company objectives are the following:

Go public. Some entrepreneurs set their company sights on going public. To them, going public accomplishes several desirable goals simultaneously. First, it furnishes a method for the outside investors to cash out and achieve the capital gain they were looking for when they invested. Second, it enables the company to raise funds needed to fuel further growth. And third, it lets the general public know that the company and its founders have reached a major milestone. Going public is a reasonable juncture signaling the departure of a starting pitcher or a milestone in the life of the professional entrepreneur. Inventor-researcher entrepreneurs with the good sense to bring in experienced executives can also aspire to this goal.

Become a giant. This is probably the most common fantasy of entrepreneurs. They figure their company will experience phenomenal growth and become a major corporation. In other words, it will become another Xerox, Polaroid, or Digital Equipment. It's a common objective because it's a glamorous objective. Professional entrepreneurs are best off in a company headed in this direction.

However, the business plan's details must prove that this objective is realistic. Usually this is done most convincingly by documenting the previous business experiences of the founders; those who have previously started successful companies or managed effectively in large companies make the most effective cases. Corporate managers who have successfully helped guide a new product or service to market or started a new division are likeliest to impress financiers.

Without such persuasive documentation, the entire document loses credibility and becomes something of a joke. (Very few ventures ever reach such levels, and it's usually not realistic to begin seriously contemplating attaining such status until after the company has gone public.)

Be acquired. Companies can be started with the explicit goal that they'll be acquired five to ten years down the road, after they've become accepted in the marketplace, have shown a pattern of steady and impressive growth, and have become profitable. The acquirer can be a major corporation, a smaller diversified company, or a group of investors looking to take over a promising growth business. This is a good situation for the starting pitcher who wants to move on or the have-your-cake-and-eat-it-too entrepreneur, who will stay on after the acquisition. Venture capitalists also will understand and approve this goal, since it offers a realistic pathway to cash out, achieving the desired capital appreciation.

Be a niche company. Some companies adeptly carve out a narrow slice of a market—some specialty component or service—that wouldn't interest many other competitors. They grow perhaps 10% or 20% annually in sales and profits and reach anywhere between $5 million and $20 million of sales. The founders are satisfied with the challenge of managing such a venture and steadily improving the product or adding an occasional new product.

Such a company can be appropriate to either the professional entrepreneur or the inventor-researcher entrepreneur. It may be of interest to private investors or lenders, but it usually doesn't excite venture capitalists unless it can be shown that they can cash out in three to seven years with appropriate capital appreciation.

Be a cash cow. There's no rule that says companies must continually grow in sales and profits. Companies can be started with the objective of getting them to a certain point in annual sales, say $1 million to $10 million, and then milking the profits. The profits might be used to support the owners' lavish lifestyles or to start or acquire other ventures. Either the lifestyle entrepreneur or the starting pitcher might seek such a situation. The starting pitcher can move on, but she or he must continue to use the cash-cow business as a type of long-term annuity.

Become a partner in a joint venture. For a young venture requiring heavy product development and marketing expenses, a major corporation's financial and marketing depth can be a powerful and attractive requirement. Becoming involved with a large company as a partner in a joint venture will give a new business instant credibility and resources.

In one instance, a company seeking $1 million of funding to build a prototype of a specialized and expensive machine to improve productivity in the semiconductor manufacturing process was advised at an MIT Enterprise Forum session to explore joint venture possibilities; such a venture was necessary to give the company the financial credibility it needed to eventually sell equipment priced in the $2 million range, panelists argued.

But negotiating joint venture agreements can be a tedious and lengthy process, and it thus needs to be well planned as an objective. This is a possible spot for the professional entrepreneur as well as the inventor-researcher entrepreneur who is adept at dealing and working closely with corporate types (or who can find a negotiator to perform this service). It's a possibility for the starting pitcher, but only if there's some provision for this individual to sell out a few years down the road.

Become a licensing company. Just as there is no rule that companies must continually grow, there is no rule that new companies must be involved in production and marketing of the products they develop. A legitimate company objective can be to constantly develop new products, processes, or services which are then licensed to others in return for a royalty on sales or for a share in a joint venture.

Inventor-researchers and lifestyle entrepreneurs sometimes take this route, concentrating their efforts on coming up with patentable products and letting others worry about getting them into the marketplace. They essentially build research and development companies, many of which are highly successful. However, obtaining financing requires highly sophisticated investors—and usually an outstanding track record as well as some developments ready or nearly ready to be licensed, plus prospective identifiable licensees.

Acquire other companies. Some companies develop into acquisition specialists, building up mini-conglomerates. They may specialize in acquiring financially troubled smaller companies and turning them around. Or they may prefer profitable companies in certain broad industry types, such as communications or transportation. Thermo-Electron Corp., a Boston-area high-technology company, used funds it received from going public to acquire other companies that were highly profitable (Lodding Engineering, Holcroft, and others), in addition to expanding from within. Once again, this is a good spot for the professional entrepreneur, since it's usually a long-term situation. (Thermo-Electron's sales now exceed $250 million annually.)

Prospective business owners do themselves a big favor personally when they decide what kind of entrepreneur they want to be and what sort of company they want to develop. Moreover, they do their business plans a big favor if they are explicit about having reconciled their personal and company objectives. They can then present a credible and desirable package to prospective investors.

One entrepreneur who appeared at an MIT Enterprise Forum session did an effective job of demonstrating such a reconciliation in his plan for a company that would act as manufacturer's representative for a variety of electronic products. The company would, after establishing itself in one to two years, evolve into a company which specialized in acquiring proprietary products from Asia to market under its own brand. In five years, the founder explained, he hoped to sell the business to a large corporation.

Aside from the market and other realities of the proposal, his statement of individual and company objectives was convincing to panelists because he had previously been an individual manufacturer's representative selling related products and he had a goal for what the company would accomplish in the near term—within two years—and in the long term—five years ahead.

We advocate that the founders summarize their objectives as a management team briefly but precisely in the business plan. This summary should be contained within the business plan's description of the company and its management's objectives (usually Section 1 in the plan).

How does one make all this convincing in the business plan? One way is by relating the entrepreneurs' previous experience to the venture they are currently starting. The most persuasive indication is a previous track record—a successful starting up of one or two companies or the development of a similar product or service for a large corporation.

When the earlier experience doesn't seem to match up logically with what is being proposed, financiers become concerned. Thus, the individuals seeking to start the fast-growing consulting firm described at the beginning of this chapter provoked skepticism among potential investors because they had no previous experience either working in a fast-growing company or developing the kinds of data-base products they were proposing as a basis for the new company.

The tendency by investors to use previous history helps explain why managers in fast-growing, high-technology companies frequently go off on their own and successfully obtain venture capital despite not having ever started a company before. These individuals have been through the growth company experience, and their desire to do the same thing on their own often rings true to investors. Similarly, executives with established airlines have leveraged their corporate experience to obtain financing for such upstarts as New York Air and People Express.

Convincingly stating the company's objectives—for instance, that it will be an acquisition candidate five years down the road or will go public in four years—not only reassures potential investors that the entrepreneurs are planning ahead, but also that they've thought about how the investors will realize their gains, which is an absolute *must* in their planning.

What Are the Industry Realities?

If there's a place where entrepreneurs get bogged down in the what-do-I-want-to-be-when-I-grow-up process, it's in matching their individual and company objectives to industry realities. Once again, the opening example of this chapter is a case in point. The consulting industry tends to be one of lifestyle entrepreneurs with typical cash-cow businesses (as defined on page 53). There are some notable exceptions, of course—Arthur D. Little and McKinsey & Company, for instance—but even these gradually evolved into substantial companies rather than starting out to be fast-growth candidates.

By virtue of seeking a substantial amount of investment funds to be a fast-growing consulting firm, the owners in this chapter's opening example were attempting to challenge their industry's pattern and experience. This isn't to say that such a business couldn't be started and succeed as they envisioned, rather that doing so in this industry would be much more difficult than in other types of industries in which such experience is common.

Two other examples from the MIT Enterprise Forum help illustrate the problem of pursuing goals inappropriate to an industry. In one case, entrepreneurs wanted to establish an information-retrieval service to compete with the Source, a fast-growing company owned by *Reader's Digest* in that developing industry. The new company was seeking $500,000 of financing, and at the time of its Enterprise Forum appearance it had no subscriptions for its service.

Panel members were quick to point out that the Source was then spending about $1 million monthly on advertising alone. Thus, attempting to become a viable competitor with a *total* of only $500,000 was like "playing penny ante in a $20 poker game," said one panelist. Or, to use another analogy, such an approach isn't unlike trying to start an automobile manufacturing company on a shoestring. The costs of entry are so high that it was quixotic or suicidal to try to enter the "videotext" industry on a low budget.

At the other extreme was an entrepreneur with a successful newsletter publishing business who approached the Enterprise Forum's executive committee for advice on his proposal to raise investment funds to acquire a magazine publishing concern. At that time, the newsletter was bringing in about $500,000 of annual revenues, of which the owner was taking out $200,000 a year in income. But he had suddenly gotten the itch to turn his cash cow into a public or giant company.

The executive committee members made two arguments against his proposal. First, they told him he would disrupt a very appealing business and personal situation with the problems of significant cash outlays to increase production and circulation along with major staffing and hiring decisions. Second, and more important, they advised him that his new dream of turning his newsletter company into something much larger was unrealistic, since the newsletter-magazine business isn't typically a $50 million- or $100 million-a-year business.

He took their advice and continues to live the good life off his solid newsletter business. And he sleeps well at night.

In both cases the message is the same. Entrepreneurs, in deciding what they want their companies to become, must examine closely what's typical in their industry. And they must explain in their business plan the common practices of others in the industry, pointing out how the new business fits the industry norms.

Sophisticated investors, bankers, and corporate executives make it a point to acquaint themselves with industry practices and will question business plans which deviate significantly from accepted procedures. This subject of industry practices and procedures is treated in greater detail in succeeding chapters.

Entrepreneurs may find exceptions—large companies flourishing in a small-company industry, or vice versa—but investors aren't usually interested in the exceptions. They want to know what the rule is. If you want to start a business that's going to be the exception, they reason, use your own money—or prove beyond reasonable doubt that you are correct and the experts are not. (It's been done, but rarely.)

Understanding Investors' and Lenders' Goals

Once entrepreneurs have determined their personal and company objectives along with what's appropriate to their industry, they must satisfy one last set of criteria: the goals of financiers.

Because many entrepreneurs tend to think first of going to venture capitalists, it's useful to begin by assessing their objectives. Most venture capitalists seek returns on the funds they invest of between 35% and 60%, compounded annually. Using 50% as an average and looking ahead five years, they expect their investment to have increased by about seven-and-one-half times (investment dollars $\times$ 1.5^n, where n equals number of years). That is, 1.5 is multiplied by itself as many times as the number of years being considered.

Venture capitalists also want an allowance for inflation, which, at a 10% annual rate, ups the 50% return to 60% (and 1.5 in the equation becomes 1.6).

An example helps illustrate the problem such objectives pose to many young companies. When a specialized software company was seeking to raise $1.8 million of financing, an MIT Enterprise Forum panelist assessed the company's case for venture capital this way:

> Your business plan says you are seeking an investment of $1.8 million. Your plan also says that in five years the company will have total sales of $11.2 million. If you make the assumption—which you have not done but should do in your business plan—that your business will be about equal in value at that time to a year's sales, then it will be worth about $11.2 million. Now venture capitalists want their investments to appreciate about 50% each year.
>
> That means that five years out, the venture capitalist is looking to cash out and receive between five and ten times the money that was put in. Let's take five—a more conservative number. Five times $1.8 million comes to $9 million in 1983 dollars. Now if you assume 5% inflation per year, which I think is much lower than what may happen between now and 1988, the investment has to be worth something on the order of $12 million to the venture capitalist. If the inflation rate is 10%, which is more likely, you'll be looking at something like $16 million or $17 million.
>
> But since your business is worth $11.2 million, you can't get there from here. The venture capitalist has to own 140% or more of your business as soon as this investment is made.

Why is there such a big emphasis on a 35% to 60% compounded annual real return? Because most money managers can earn 20% on their money by investing in established listed stocks and other "safe" securities. Startup and early-stage companies are far from established or safe and are likely to encounter various financial and managerial problems, any one of which could lead to failure.

The reward thus has to be commensurate with the risk and, from that viewpoint, a 50% return is a standard venture (risk) capital objective. This is the risk/reward relationship that applies to venture investments.

There are, of course, other kinds of investors besides venture capitalists. Under relaxed Securities and Exchange Commission rules it's now possible to assemble groups of private investors more easily than was once the case.

It's also possible to take a two- or three-year-old company public. Indeed, founders of the specialized software company just examined might have done well to explore that possibility because, "The public is not as sophisticated as a venture capitalist," according to a Forum panelist. Thus, it might be possible to raise public funds without talking about a rate of return that venture capitalists would demand. However, the unsophisticated investor has also become litigious. Investor lawsuits often follow public offerings that are not wildly profitable, so beware.

Another financing option includes lenders—banks, commercial finance firms, government agencies—which have objectives quite different from those of investors. Lenders are primarily concerned that whatever they loan out must be repaid. So in assessing whether or not to grant a loan, their first hard and fast rule is to require collateral—machinery, inventory, buildings. That way, if the business fails, the lenders can sell the collateral and have the loan repaid from the proceeds.

Because Nancy C.'s company, mentioned in Chapter 1, was already several years old, it might have been a candidate for a bank or other loan as well. It could have used equipment or orders on its books as collateral.

Since startup companies typically don't have much in the way of collateral, it's up to the principals to supply it out of their personal assets to obtain bank or other loans. The collateral might be in the form of the owners' homes, life insurance, or stocks. Entrepreneurs should be aware, though, that there exist some horror stories of homes lost and financial credibility destroyed through such pledges of collateral.

Tailoring a Coherent Tale

All four of the issues that are part of the growing-up question must in a sense be made to intersect appropriately in the business plan. That is, investors or lenders must get a sense that entrepreneurs know what they want for themselves and for their company and that their objectives are appropriate, credible, and provable, both to their industry and to the financiers approached.

If the tale isn't coherent and doesn't ring true, investors will resist. That helps explain the criticism encountered by the fledgling consulting firm described at the beginning of this chapter. The entrepreneurs, by failing to provide any sense of how venture capitalists might liquidate their investment (cash out) and by attempting to be an exception to their industry's growth pattern, made investors wonder whether their overall objectives had been thoroughly thought through.

If the consultants truly aspired to be professional entrepreneurs guiding a fast-growing business, they couldn't expect much in the way of either investor or lender help in their early stages. Investors would shy away because of confusion over the reality of the principals' and company's objectives, and lenders would resist because no collateral exists (unless the principals decide to pledge personal assets).

Thus, their only hope might be to bootstrap the business, perhaps getting customers to finance a data-gathering effort and in that way begin establishing a record of impressive growth. Once they have a track record, their goals would be-- come more believable and convincing, and venture capital could be a possibility (provided they could satisfy all of the other venture capital criteria).

Fledgling companies, then, must be able to assess where they want themselves and their companies to go over the coming five years in terms of what is realistic to expect. We have considered this five-year planning process in terms of the individual, the company, industry realities, and financiers' goals; subsequent chapters examine other aspects of this planning process.

When all aspects of the growing-up tale don't fit together into a coherent story, adjustments must be made. The specialized software company, for instance, was advised to reduce the amount of investment funds it was seeking so as to make the potential returns more attractive to investors. If that was impractical, another alternative, panelists said, was simply to bootstrap the operation and look toward making it a cash cow.

What do you want to be when you grow up? It's never an easy question to answer, for individuals or for companies. But investors want to know, and the business plan must contain a believable answer. Most important: Bear in mind that today's investors employ skilled staff people, consultants, and investigators who will engage in a "due diligence" process to check out each and every important statement, projection, and assertion made in the business plan—as well as the entrepreneurs' own background, integrity, and history. Any exaggeration or misstatement will be recorded and somehow incorporated into the investment community's informal "data bank" for future reference.

IN SUMMARY

Entrepreneurs must articulate clearly and concisely in Section 1 of the business plan the goals of the management team and company looking five years ahead. Arriving at a convincing statement of goals entails going through a four-step process of evaluation as follows:

• Self-assessment by the founders. What do they want for themselves personally and financially five years down the road in terms of their interests, wishes, and needs? Among the alternatives are to be a starting pitcher, a professional entrepreneur, and a lifestyle entrepreneur.

• Stating of the company objectives. How can the founders' personal-financial goals be transformed into a realistic venture? Among the alternatives are to go public, become a giant, be acquired, be a niche company, and be a cash cow.

• Matching of individual and company objectives to industry realities. How realistic are these objectives in terms of what ordinarily occurs in the venture's industry? Financiers don't like to back companies which expect to be the exceptions to the industry trends.

• Satisfying of financiers' goals. How well do the venture goals mesh with investor and lender financing criteria? Investors must obtain specific investment returns, and lenders must ensure repayment of loans. Entrepreneurs must satisfy the criteria of the financiers approached.

4

What's the User Benefit and Other Marketing Issues

Effectively exploiting markets is the key to unlocking the doors to commercial success. This chapter advises entrepreneurs about how they can demonstrate that they focus on appropriate marketing issues so as to effectively complete Section 2 of the business plan, "Markets and Competition" (see the sample table of contents on page 32).

Among the issues this chapter considers are defining and quantifying user benefit, establishing the market size and potential customer interest, and assessing the competition. Entrepreneurs must tackle these issues convincingly because investors want to put their money into "market-driven" companies rather than "technology-driven" or service-driven companies. That is, the attractiveness to investors of market and sales potential is far more important than the attractiveness of the product or service and its technical features.

This is a very basic notion, but it's an easy one for even the experts to overlook or forget, as a recent presentation at the MIT Enterprise Forum made clear. The entrepreneur's talk was fairly typical as he spent the bulk of his twenty-minute presentation period extolling his company's product—an instrument for use in the textile industry to control certain aspects of the production process. He rounded out his talk with some financial projections looking five years down the road.

The first panelist to react to the business plan—a partner in a venture capital firm—was completely negative about the company's prospects for obtaining investment funds because, he stated, its market essentially consisted of a depressed industry; at that time, the textile industry was performing poorly.

Another panelist then asked the presenter, "How long does it take your product to pay for itself in decreased production costs?" The presenter immediately responded, "Six months."

This second panelist told the entrepreneur: "That's the most important thing you've said tonight."

The venture capitalist who had originally been negative quickly reversed himself. He would back a company in almost any industry, however depressed, he said, if the enterprise could prove, and emphasize in its sales approach, that such an important user benefit existed—that the product would recover the customer's cost in six months. Despite the venture capitalist's temporary lapse, he knew that anyone selling instruments, machinery, or services which will pay for themselves in less than one year essentially are mandatory purchases for many potential customers within a market. If the payback period is less than two years, it's still a probable purchase. If the payback is beyond three years, forget it.

The panel advised the presenter to recast his business plan and oral presentation to emphasize the fact that the company's products pay for themselves in less than one year and de-emphasize the self-serving discussion about the innovation and technological advances incorporated in the product. The presenter was extremely grateful and said that, from his viewpoint, the company had been turned around by this shift in emphasis.

Indeed, the presenter revised the business plan so that the company began emphasizing its user benefit in tangible and easily understandable terms. The company is doing very well, having successfully made the transition from being a technology-driven company to being a market-driven one.

On Being Customer Oriented

If there is one theme that recurs more than any other at MIT Enterprise Forum sessions, it is the theme of user benefit. For all the talk about investors' interest in glamorous high-technology businesses, they are even more interested in entrepreneurs who demonstrate basic marketing skills, the most important of which is an understanding and appreciation of the benefit to the user of a company's products or services. That is, how will the customer profit or otherwise gain from using the seller's product or service? Ideally, this benefit can be quantified to show that the customer will save the cost of the product or service in a specified amount of time.

Essentially, user benefit is one of the most convincing points entrepreneurs can make to prove that sales will be made, cash will flow, and profits will result. Explaining user benefit enables the business plan to clearly demonstrate that the company has perceived a bona fide need in the marketplace and that it can convince its prospective customers to purchase its products or services—immediately.

The notion of user benefit is one that is actually an essential part of modern marketing theory, which holds that to sell effectively, companies must first understand what customers really want. That is, sellers must offer products and services which help and please customers. As obvious as that basic idea may seem, entrepreneurs—and even investors, as we just described—have a way of forgetting or ignoring it. Instead, they get wrapped up in the special attributes of their products or services, and they neglect to consider whether such attributes are of importance to potential customers.

Nor is the tendency to overlook user benefit limited to young businesses. Many well-established companies could increase their sales substantially, we are convinced, if they more clearly and forcefully emphasized user benefit rather than simply product characteristics and specifications. We've seen product literature produced by old-line companies doing moderately well that could be made much more effective if they gave the proper emphasis to specific user benefits of the product. We are essentially advocating a change in viewpoint rather than a change in product or service.

Companies which realize the importance of this concept can make impressive sales gains. Back in the 1960s—before many banks had installed computerized accounting systems—a major business computer manufacturer decided to begin penetrating the bank market by emphasizing user benefit. Its sales team approached a very conservative bank in Hartford by analyzing the work and business load in its bookkeeping and accounting departments. The bank president agreed with the analysis and was duly impressed by the sales team's efforts to understand his bank's operations.

The computer group then demonstrated for the president that its system would enable the bank to save the price of the equipment in just one year through decreased labor costs. It demonstrated additional benefits as well, such as fewer errors and improved employee morale.

In an effort to clinch its argument, the computer group offered a money-back guarantee if the equipment failed to pay for itself in less than one year. The bank called an emergency session of its board of directors, followed by a very rapid "due diligence" effort to investigate the computer company's claims. The bank signed a purchase agreement within sixty days of the presentation, and the installation was a success.

Note that this presentation was based almost entirely upon the product's user benefits. It's also worth remembering that this event took place in the 1960s, when there was little emphasis on such things as "solid state" innovation and other razzle-dazzle. The emphasis was on benefits to the customer.

Quantifying the User Benefit

Underarm deodorant and mouthwash sellers suggest that buyers will improve their chances for friendship and romance. Yogurt makers promise an improved figure. Makers of prepared frozen dinners say buyers will save time and so gain freedom from drudgery.

As such common television commercials illustrate, user benefits can vary widely. For mass-produced consumer items, such subtle and intangible benefits can be important. But for most fledgling companies, which don't have huge advertising budgets and are catering to specialized business markets, user benefits must be more precise and preferably financial.

The most convincing user benefit, as we have suggested, is often a direct financial saving to customers. That allows sellers to calculate a "payback" period for a product or service to use as a selling point to customers.

Entrepreneurs should briefly highlight the user benefit in the business plan's executive summary and in detail in the "User Benefit" part of Section 2, "Markets and Competition." Demonstrating or calculating the payback period often isn't as obvious as it might seem. For fledgling companies selling to business customers, calculating the payback period may require consideration of the following areas:

1. *Fewer rejects, or breakdowns, in the customer's production process (increased useful yield).* A number of companies developing products to improve the process of producing semiconductor chips fall into this category.

Similarly, companies which effectively service office equipment also fall into this category. One photocopy machine repair service has done quite well by promising to reduce copier breakdowns through more extensive preventive maintenance—at the same maintenance fee that competitors offer. Users of office copiers benefit through reduced labor costs and increased productivity created from reliable copying.

A company which made a product falling into this category but didn't realize it gave a presentation at the MIT Enterprise Forum. It was seeking financing to expand sales of an instrument that would aid the semiconductor manufacturing process by reducing the time required for quality control (QC) testing and that would improve the accuracy of the measurements taken in the QC laboratory.

A panel member told the presenter, "You've described the instrument and told us what a smart piece of equipment it is. You have also said that you've sold about half a dozen of the instruments. But you haven't defined exactly why the customer buys it from you. Can you quantify the user benefit in dollars?"

The presenter responded by saying that the hours saved per test would not justify the cost of the instrument, but that the company's few customers were extremely happy with their purchase. Further discussion established that faster and more accurate testing of samples brought in from the production line to the QC laboratory had increased the production yield (percent of product manufactured which met specifications and could be shipped to customers).

When the panel urged the presenter to probe more deeply into the increased product yield made possible by the instrument, he "guesstimated" that it allowed perhaps a 2% higher yield of usable output. Under further questioning, the presenter told the panel that the instrument was in place on a production line accounting for $5 million of shipments annually.

The user benefit then became obvious: 2% of $5 million is $100,000 per year. The instrument carried a sales tag of $5,000. That meant it had paid for itself with this particular customer in only two weeks—a tremendous user benefit. The presenter was encouraged to rewrite his product literature to emphasize the short payback period as the chief reason for buying the product. He was also encouraged to raise his price considerably before contacting every manufacturer that could make use of the company's product. After that, the company should have been in a position to simply rake in the purchase orders.

2. *Lower warranty costs.* This benefit is related to the previous one. That is, if product quality is improved, then costs associated with repairing or replacing defective products which fall into customers' hands should be reduced. If the panelists had taken the previous example a step further, they might have asked the presenter about the customer's warranty costs. Based on the improved quality, those costs should also have been reduced by at least 2%. That savings could then be calculated into the payback period, reducing it to even less than two weeks.

3. *Advantages leading to a better-quality end product (competitive advantage for one's customers).* Such advantages are often conferred by proprietary technology or processes. A presenter

at an MIT Enterprise Forum session had just such a product in an auto-theft alarm system. By making use of proprietary microelectronic circuitry, the company had come up with a product its officials argued convincingly was less prone to false alarms and more sensitive to actual theft attempts than existing alarm systems.

The payback period, then, might very well come in a single evening when one's car is parked on a dark urban street, the presenter said. "Would you leave a briefcase containing $11,000 (the value of an average car) tied to a parking meter?" asked the presenter in justifying the product's $400 price tag.

4. *Faster turnover of inventory resulting in lower storage and interest expenses.* A presenter at an MIT Enterprise Forum session described such a device—a computer-linked radio control device that would enable companies which must store large volumes of supplies, such as discount drug chains, to keep better tabs of where items are in the warehouse and which items are in ample supply and which are in short supply.

Unlike many entrepreneurs who come before the MIT Enterprise Forum, the founders of this company had gone to the trouble of calculating the number of hours, warehouse space costs, and interest expenses their product would save a typical customer by virtue of tighter inventory controls. They concluded that, for most customers, the product would save its cost in ten months. A panelist commended the presenters by observing, "The most important thing you have told us is that the system pays for itself in ten months. Not enough companies are sensitive to that aspect of user benefit. Tell your sales prospects that, after your system pays for itself in ten months, it's a money printing machine."

5. *Improved efficiency in accomplishing any number of tasks, from laboratory research to product delivery.* Another entrepreneur who had gone to the trouble of calculating the payback period appeared before the MIT Enterprise Forum with a product that would help customers save money in the area of product delivery. When hooked up to trucks, his company's device monitored such things as engine idling speed, driving speed, warm-up time, and intervals between deliveries.

The effect of the device was to enable companies which incur heavy delivery costs—such as grocery chains—to cut fuel consumption and driver overtime expenses. According to the entrepreneur, users of the product could expect to recover the $1,400 per-truck cost of the item within a year. Although one panelist felt that the calculation of payback period was too optimistic, most of the panelist comments focused on other issues unrelated to this basic marketing issue. Indeed, most indicated that the presenter's straightforward consideration of the payback period had left them extremely impressed with the product's long-term prospects.

6. *Improved convenience.* Saving time, for many customers, also means saving money. A woman who started designing clothing for professional women found this out as she began selling the items to groups of friends and acquaintances. The working women were relieved to be able to find appropriate clothing at prices comparable to retail outlets without rummaging through racks in many stores. The founder of this business took the idea of making attractive fashions readily available a step further by setting up a mail-order business, which has thrived as professional women welcome the oppor-

tunity to invest their shopping time in their professions or families.

As the previous discussion suggests, calculation of the payback period is limited in many cases only by the entrepreneur's ingenuity. For instance, the payback doesn't have to be just in terms of money saved; it can also be in terms of money earned. If a new production tool, instrument, computer, or program enables the customer to produce a better product, the user benefit can be presented in terms of increased revenues.

Thus, young companies seeking to raise investment funds must be constantly alert to possible advantages conferred by their products or services and incorporate them into both their sales literature and business plans.

Of course, all of the user benefits mentioned above are meant to complement, not replace, some of the most elementary user benefits: promotion of a product similar to that being offered by the competition, but at a lower price; or a better product at the same price; or, best of all, a better product at a lower price.

Young companies which accomplish this last goal—for instance, using a technical innovation to manufacture an existing product for 30% less than competitors can—should emphasize as the user benefit the prospect of buying the same product at an immediate 30% discount. They should emphasize in the business plan the existing size of the market and the impact of bringing out a competitive product at a price so low that competitors would be squeezed down to little or no profit to match it.

Investors will probably be impressed by the decreased cost of the product to the user's customers, since it makes likely significant market penetration as soon as prospective customers learn of the new entrant's benefits.

Somewhat more difficult to establish is the user benefit for a new product which has superior characteristics at the same price as established products. Entrepreneurs can learn from prospective customers about likely benefits, since they are usually highly receptive toward product improvements which can lead to other benefits.

Entrepreneurs mustn't lose sight of the limitations conferred by price and quality advantages, however. For instance, a startup company which made a presentation to the MIT Enterprise Forum had a seemingly big winner in special material (known as wafers) it proposed to manufacture for use in the photovoltaic industry at a price 30% less than existing wafers. The photovoltaic companies use the wafers to make solar energy and microelectronic devices.

Under questioning by panelists, the presenter explained how potential customers must install new equipment to be able to use his company's wafers, since they are configured differently than existing wafers for production purposes. The 30% cost savings enables customers to recover the cost of the new equipment in four months, he noted. But the panelists weren't totally convinced.

"You're asking an entire industry to buy new equipment and change the way it manufactures its existing products," a panelist observed. "That's hard to do, especially for a startup company." The panelist advised the entrepreneur to systematically survey potential customers about whether they would be willing to make the changes necessary to buy the new product and to include the results of the inquiry in the business plan to convince investors that the market exists—and is truly receptive.

To sum up, then, managers seeking to quantify the user benefit of their product or service should ask themselves the following questions:

1. How much does it save the customer? Savings can come through reduced labor costs, lowered reject rate, reduced downtime, lowered inventory costs, and improved convenience.

2. How much does it earn the customer? Earnings can come through heightened productivity, improved product performance, and increased productive capacity.

3. What non-monetary benefits do customers realize? These can include entertainment, improved appearance, and better health. Although these are difficult to quantify financially, they can be identified and described in the business plan, often as complements to more easily quantifiable benefits.

Is There Really a Market Out There?

As important a step as calculating the user benefit is, it's still only a step, and a first step at that. Assuming that a substantial user benefit exists—say, a payback period of less than a year—there must still be evidence of enough potential buyers to predict (realistically) sales in volumes attractive to investors.

Thus, the business plan must address the very basic question—Is there really a market out there for the product at the price and in the package proposed? Addressing that question involves, essentially, a two-step process, as follows:

1. *Evidence of marketplace interest.* Entrepreneurs must show in the business plan that customer prospects have given clearly positive responses to the question, "Having heard our pitch,

will you buy?" Investments will not be made unless the answer to this question is a strong "Yes."

How can startup businesses, some of which may only have a prototype product or an idea for a service, appropriately answer that question? A presenter at an MIT Enterprise Forum session posed just that issue to panelists not long ago. His company had put together a prototype of a device that fits into personal computers and allows them to handle telephone messages. The company needed to demonstrate that customers would buy the product, but the company had exhausted its cash resources and was thus unable to build and sell the item in quantity.

Panelists offered two possible approaches. First, the founders might allow a few likely customers to use the prototype and obtain written testimonials from them as to their evaluation of the product and possible interest when it becomes available as a standard product.

Second, the founders might offer the product to a few potential customers at a substantial price discount, provided the customers would pay part of the cost—say one-third—upfront to enable the company to build the product. That would allow the venture not only to show that potential buyers exist but to demonstrate the product to potential investors in real-life installations.

The same philosophy applies to a proposed new service. It might be offered at a discount to initial customers as a form of prototype in return for an agreement that the customer will serve as a reference in marketing the service to others.

Services, of course, can frequently be launched on a small scale so as to build up a base of possible referrals. When a secretary at a university business school decided to start her own secretarial word processing business, she opened the of-

fice near the school, where she had previously done much
free-lance typing and had many satisfied customers to whom
she could refer potential non-university customers.

For new products, though, nothing at this point succeeds so
well as letters of support and appreciation from some significant potential customers along with a "reference installation"
or two. Third-party statements, from would-be or demonstration customers, initial users, sales representatives, or distributors, can be successfully employed to support the conten-
tion that the company has indeed discovered a sound market
and that the product or service will be needed and marketed
successfully.

In one particular case, which preceded the Enterprise
Forum by a decade, a startup company which proposed to
manufacture a physical device to control foam and aeration in
various industrial liquids was seeking investment funds to enable it to market its product, which had already been engineered and installed in certain test applications.

A group of venture capitalists, who were intrigued with the
new company, inquired of the founders, "Have you ever installed one of these systems? Your business plan looks interesting, but this is an entirely new approach, and we have no
way of evaluating how customers might feel about it."

The founders quickly arranged for the potential investors
and a consultant whose services they had engaged to fly to one
of the sites in which the system had been installed and was in
operation. The entrepreneurs wisely asked the venture capitalists to raise any questions they might have with the plant
manager; the founders then removed themselves from the discussion. The plant manager told the group that the product
had paid for itself in less than four months and that he was so
delighted with it that he planned to purchase additional units.

The venture capitalists made their investment within five weeks!

Letters from users can be obtained, even if the product is only in prototype form. It can be installed experimentally to prove its worth. In such cases, a deal can be struck with a user, wherein the product will be sold at cost (or below) in return for information as to the specific benefits it provides and an agreement to talk to sales prospects or investors. Letters from such experimental customers attesting to the value of the product can be included in an appendix to the business plan or in a separate volume. During the "due diligence" process, investors are influenced most positively when they can check with happy users or clients, even if the installations are experimental.

Such approaches can help entrepreneurs avoid the unfortunate situation of developing a product or service that is ahead of its time. For instance, a device created in 1947 to measure the elasticity of fibers in fabrics, papers, and plastics was judged by its inventor to have a wide range of potential applications in the textile, paper, and plastics industries. Actually, the device was so far ahead of its time that the company formed to produce and sell the item passed through four owners before it became a success, nineteen years later. The company's device, which uses sound waves to measure the modulus of elasticity of fibers while they undergo various tests, has now become a standard tool in all the industries it was designed for; it just took nearly twenty years for the industrial concerns to realize what they needed. A bit of investigation of potential buyers in the 1940s would have demonstrated an extremely limited market for this product; the same investigation in the mid-1960s would have led to a quite different outcome.

2. *Documentation of market claims.* Quantitative information about the market for products or services is extremely important, since it is the basis for the financial projections which will determine whether prospective investors should become involved. Section 2 of the business plan must provide a credible estimate of the total possible number of customers and the price they are willing to pay, leading to a dollar value of the market.

Assertions about the market and the growth rate of sales and profits must be supported with carefully analyzed data rather than the usual, and not credible, generalizations, such as, "If we're smart we'll be able to get about 10% of the market," or "Even if we only get 1% of such a huge market, we'll be in good shape."

Investors know from experience that there's no guarantee a new company will get any business, regardless of market size. But if such assertions have some basis in fact—as borne out by concrete evidence of customer interest—they can quickly crumble if the data on which they are based aren't carefully gathered and analyzed.

As one example of the danger inherent in such broad statements, a business plan that came before the MIT Enterprise Forum proposed selling a service to "small businesses," calculating that, based on 17 million such enterprises in the United States, penetrating even 1% of the market should result in 170,000 sales. The problem with that analysis, a panelist familiar with the statistics on small businesses pointed out, was that anywhere from 11 million to 14 million of the so-called small businesses were really sole proprietorships or part-time businesses. Thus, the total number of full-time small businesses with employees (this company's real market) was actually between 3 million and 6 million, not 17 million. Of course, that finding altered considerably the company's projections and prospects.

Similarly, in a business plan relating to the sale of certain equipment to apple growers, U.S. Department of Agriculture statistics would be necessary to discover the number of growers who could use the equipment. If only growers with fifty acres or more could be expected to make effective use of it, then the entrepreneurs would need to determine how many growers have such size farms, as distinguished from minor producers with an acre or two of apple trees.

Thus, it is necessary to determine with reasonable certainty the number of potential customers, the size of their businesses, and which of those sizes are appropriate to the products or services being offered. Indeed, there are times when "bigger is not better." For example, a savings of $10,000 per year in chemical usage may be significant to a modest concern, but it might not be important enough for Du Pont or Monsanto to be interested.

Because the rate at which a company will grow may be based on the accessibility of its clients, entrepreneurs should take note in the business plan of where customers are likely to be located. This has become less important in our age of jet aircraft and easy telephone communication, but in certain fields it's a serious factor. For instance, semiconductor companies should be near either Silicon Valley in California or Route 128 near Boston. Businesses which sell to manufacturers of women's clothing should be based in New York City. Businesses providing services to wine growers should be in California. That enables sellers to easily make many sales calls per day. If likely customers are difficult to reach, appropriate travel costs should be factored into the marketing strategy.

The marketing research should also consider the nature of the industry being addressed. For instance, few industries are as conservative as banks and public utilities. Although there are a relatively small number of potential customers, all of which are clearly identified and known, their acceptance of new products or services, even those thoroughly proven, is painfully slow. Both entrepreneurs and their investors must be extremely patient. Yet such industries can be attractive because, while banks and utilities do act slowly, they also have the buying power to make the wait worthwhile.

At the other end of the spectrum are extremely fast growing, and fast changing, industries, such as franchised weight-loss clinics and computer software companies. Here the problem is reversed. Although some such companies have become multimillion-dollar firms in just a few years, their sales are vulnerable to declines of similar proportions if their offerings are superseded by competitors. Under such conditions, it's necessary to produce the product or service being sold to the industry so rapidly that potential competitors will be discouraged from entering the marketplace.

These extreme examples are provided to point out the necessity of convincingly projecting the rate of acceptance for the product or service and the rate at which it will likely be sold. From this marketing research data, the sales plan will emerge in orderly fashion. (We cover details of the sales plan in the next chapter.) At the same time, much of the internal structure of the fledgling business—in terms of plant and staff—will be geared to the sales and marketing requirements.

At this point, we hasten to add that evidence and data supporting a company's optimism about its product or service should only be summarized in the main body of the business plan. The marketing section of the plan shouldn't exceed ten pages, with the details collected in an appendix or in a separate volume if such data is extensive. We favor the separate volume approach because it allows much supporting information to be included in a non-obtrusive way. The second volume is usually turned over to staff investigators by the venture capital firm for use in the "due diligence" process.

A business plan which integrates the internal and external marketing pressures on the company will be viewed by investors as evidence of a competent and mature management team and will invite serious consideration. By contrast, omission of such factors will be viewed as evidence that the company is not market-driven and probably should not be given serious consideration for investment.

The Nature and Number of Products

When it comes to marketing, originality and quantity aren't always desirable characteristics. It's often more difficult to sell a new product or service than an improved version of an existing one.

A case that came before the MIT Enterprise Forum helps illustrate this point. A company comprised of four engineers had developed half a dozen new products based on laser technology; the venture was seeking investment funds to market the products. The panelists appreciated the sophistication of the technology the engineers were using, but they were concerned, first, about market acceptance of the products and, second, about whether the entrepreneurs were seeking to do too much too soon.

As much as it may pain innovators, investors know that it is easier to sell products or services in an established field in which demand for a product category already exists rather than in a totally new area in which it is first necessary to establish a demand for the product. That is, well-established fields enable newcomers to show substantial user benefit, evidence of product acceptance, and data to accurately describe the potential market size.

Although it is more difficult, it is not impossible to attract investors and make sales in a new field in which demand must first be created before the field can really exist. Being aware of a potential investor's concerns and objections when dealing in a new area may enable the entrepreneur to appropriately address and possibly overcome them in the business plan and following presentations.

And as we noted in Chapter 1, marketing and sales considerations should show clear evidence of concentration and focus. Some entrepreneurs think that investors will consider them to be better risks if they attempt to develop and market ten new products instead of one. Their thinking is based on the oil-well–drilling mentality, in which ten wells are drilled, hoping that three will come in. The three good wells will more than cover the expenses associated with the seven dry wells. As logical as such philosophy sounds, it is not the way investors think. They want solid evidence that the one well entrepreneurs are digging will yield oil.

Two entrepreneurs who took that approach had a small auto repair business, which they wanted to expand quickly so as to generate increased revenues. Their approach was to assemble a business plan which promised four "profit centers"— auto repair, auto rental, long-term leasing, and used-car sales. Potential lenders saw those profit centers as potential loss centers, and they refused financing.

Indeed, nothing will drive investors away more quickly than the idea that management will waste its time, and their money, trying to market too many products at once. As a rule of thumb, a company doing $1 million or less annual sales should only have one product. A company doing $2 million to $3 million could support two products. A company would need annual sales in excess of $25 million to do justice to ten products.

As every practical businessman knows, it takes considerable time and energy to pay proper attention to even a single line of products. Any budding entrepreneur who thinks that he or she will score points with investors by planning to launch many products at once is in for a rude awakening. Concentration and focus will win favor and investment.

The Competition

No business plan is credible unless it includes a realistic appraisal of the company's competition. There's no sense attempting to conceal the company's relative position in the marketplace. Interested investors are certain to discover the real competitive situation during the "due diligence" process, when they investigate the company's competitors, their products and services, their pricing, their warranty policies, and the way they are viewed by customers.

Since most entrepreneurs are already familiar with the industry in which they are proposing to begin a business, assessing the competition usually isn't difficult. They can obtain sales literature, talk with customers, and inquire of purchasing agents, sales representatives, and others about their assessments of competitors.

When a team of four entrepreneurs was preparing a business plan to acquire and remodel a restaurant on Cape Cod, they decided that an effective way to demonstrate the superiority of their revamping ideas was to assess the competition. So they visited all restaurants within a five-mile radius and took note of their menu offerings and prices, type of cuisine, hours, attitudes of customers, and other factors, and they summarized their findings. That assessment of the competition helped the founders win a Small Business Administration loan.

Similarly, when three entrepreneurs were assembling a business plan for a newsletter, they began receiving two newsletters they considered to be their most direct competitors. The newsletters and accompanying sales promotion literature enabled the individuals to describe their competitors' prices, promotion, and product strengths and weaknesses, and it helped them win investment funds.

Failure to be forthright about such information makes a young company appear both negligent and dishonest. Therefore, entrepreneurs must take care in the marketing section of the business plan to describe the competition and explain how their company is superior to others already in the marketplace.

Besides impressing investors, entrepreneurs stand to gain another benefit from investigating the competition—learning how they present their financials and apportion their resources. Such insight can be useful in evaluating whether projections about income and expense trends are realistic, based on industry practices.

Marketing versus Sales

Finally, in assembling a marketing section of the business plan, entrepreneurs must make a clear distinction between marketing and sales. Too often, entrepreneurs see the two as identical. Simply stated, marketing is strategy and sales are tactics. The marketing section of the business plan identifies the user benefits, the likely buyers, trends in the marketplace, and the nature of the competition, among various strategic issues. This distinction—and how to develop it in the business plan—is the subject of the next chapter.

IN SUMMARY

Entrepreneurs must convey in the business plan a strong sense of being marketing oriented. In writing the marketing section of the plan, managers should address the following issues:

• What is the product's or service's user benefit? That is, how long will it take for the product or service to pay for itself? The more quickly it does, the more likely it is to appeal to customers.

• What evidence is there of marketplace interest? It is preferred that this should be demonstrated by potential customers buying or using early versions of the product or service. It should also be supported with data about the size and buying habits of the targeted market.

• What is the nature and number of products and services? Most preferable are improvements on existing offerings and focus on one or a few products or services.

• What is the nature of the competition? Business plans must describe competitors in terms of their prices, marketing approaches, quality, and other characteristics.

5

Selling and Supporting Your Product

A company described at a 1984 MIT Enterprise Forum session by its president, Stephen H., obviously had a lot going for it. Its specialized equipment for microcomputer manufacturers gave it a dual advantage: several proprietary products in a growth industry. It expected its 1983 sales of $1.2 million to double to $2.4 million in 1984. The company was looking for $950,000 of venture capital to enable it to expand its facilities and develop new products in order to achieve $22 million of sales five years down the road, with pre-tax profit margins of 20%, according to Stephen.

Unlike many other entrepreneurs who appear at the Enterprise Forum, Stephen even offered ideas about the products' user benefits. By virtue of enabling computer manufacturers to improve their productivity and to do custom design quickly, his company's products should pay for themselves within a year, he indicated.

The panelists were impressed, except for one primary concern: the company's plan for selling its products to produce the $22 million of sales five years hence.

"You have a good broad marketing plan," said one panelist. "It covers all the important areas. There's just not enough detail on your selling organization. Who are the people doing the selling? Where are they located? How are they organized? How are they expected to perform and how are they compensated? How do your competitors sell their products?"

As this panelist suggested, logically and convincingly addressing the marketing issues described in the previous chapter is only half the battle insofar as the marketing aspects of the business plan are concerned. The other half is thoroughly and appropriately explaining in the business plan how the company's product or service will be sold and promoted and, moreover, how that sales-promotion effort will be supervised and monitored.

Essentially, the marketing issues of the previous chapter might be viewed as matters of strategy. The selling and support issues of this chapter are matters of tactics. Once entrepreneurs have described where their product or service fits into the marketplace—how much it will save customers, what the size of the market is, who the competitors are—they must be able to detail exactly how they'll go about getting their offering into customers' hands. This description comprises Section 4 of the business plan, "Selling." (See the sample table of contents beginning on page 32.)

Too often, entrepreneurs provide impressive descriptions of their products and the huge markets that await them, but they neglect to deal with the nuts and bolts of how the products will be sold and supported. Such failure creates two kinds of doubts in investors' minds. On a general level, they wonder whether the entrepreneurs have done their homework. More specifically, potential investors worry that a company will be product-driven—that the entrepreneurs have not planned the specific methods and resources needed to produce sales, cash flow, and the profits that are the only real motivation for investors.

Some companies, at least at an early stage of industry development, can afford to be product-driven. The minicomputer and personal computer industries were that way early on, as customers sought out Digital Equipment and Data General minicomputers and Apple and Sinclair personal computers. Similarly, in the service area, fast-food franchises such as McDonald's and weight-loss-clinic franchises such as Weight Watchers grew quickly as the ideas behind both caught on.

But once industries mature and market-driven competitors become involved, selling tactics become extremely important. Investors want to feel comfortable that the companies they back will be similarly marketing oriented; the best way for investors to reassure themselves is to see a detailed and sensible description of selling, promotion, and support tactics.

The remainder of this chapter will provide guidance for assembling the sales and support aspects of the business plan.

Appropriate Distribution Channels

A first step in assembling a convincing sales plan is deciding how the product or service will be sold. To many entrepreneurs, selling means simply hiring a sales force. But investors view the sales process differently and have their own set of criteria for determining the most effective ways of selling, which include executive selling, in-house sales forces, sales representatives, distributors, direct mail, and retailing, all of which are described in this chapter.

To illustrate, take the case of an entrepreneur who appeared before the MIT Enterprise Forum and described at some length how his company would sell its specialized computer software for about $2,000 a program. What was his selling approach? He would hire a sales force to aggressively push the product.

A panelist quickly dispensed with that idea. He explained that an appropriate allowance to support the cost of each sale is 10% of the selling price. For a $2,000 product, that would leave about $200 to cover the costs associated with the salesperson—salary, commission, benefits, and travel expenses. That might seem a reasonable amount, the panelist explained, except that the salesperson isn't going to sell an item to every prospect. If one out of every five prospects winds up buying, the amount available per sales call suddenly drops to only $40 ($200 divided by five).

"A traveling salesperson may spend an hour or two calling on each prospect, between travel and waiting time and the actual presentation," the panelist explained. "There's no way $40 will be enough to cover a sales call. You have to figure a salesperson's expenses at $100 an hour at least."

For this particular product, the panelist argued, the entrepreneur would need to come up with another means of distribution. "Probably the most appropriate way of selling a $2,000 product is through independent sales representatives, who can afford a $40 allotment per sales call because they are selling other companies' items at the same time," the panelist explained. (Sales representatives will generally seek to sell the products of between eight and twelve companies to each prospect, increasing both the frequency and volume of the representatives' sales and lowering the cost to each selling company of individual sales calls.)

If the software product had a $20,000 price tag, another panelist observed, then the idea of a sales force might make sense. In that situation, 10% of the price would allow a $2,000 cost for each sale. And figuring that five prospects must be called to make one sale would still allow $400 per call—an affordable cost.

This investor rationale about selling costs helps explain why various services and products are sold as they are. Professional seminars costing a few hundred dollars per participant are sold via mass mailings, while an airline ticket for $150 or $200 is sold by travel agents representing many airlines.

IBM has thousands of salespeople selling its mainframe computers and minicomputers, most of which are priced in excess of $40,000. But IBM, for the most part, won't allow its sales force to sell the IBM Personal Computer (IBM PC), preferring to distribute it through independent or company-owned computer stores. That's because the IBM PC sells for about $3,000, which isn't enough to cover the costs of selling door-to-door.

The only way an IBM salesperson can sell the IBM PC is in quantities of at least twenty, such as to corporations. Selling in such quantities raises the purchase price to about $60,000 minimum, which makes it worth an in-house salesperson's costs to sell.

Similarly, other low-priced goods and services which normally wouldn't justify a sales force might do so if they are sold in quantity. Examples include electronic components, equipment parts, office supplies, personnel services, and seminar programs for large numbers of a single company's employees.

Or, low-priced items can be sold by a personal sales force if the sellers are part-time individuals seeking to earn extra cash rather than support a household. Avon, Amway, and Tupperware depend on such part-time individuals, who often seek sales experience and social outlets as much or more than they do earnings.

At the other extreme, entrepreneurs whose companies' products or services are especially high priced—say, production machinery or specialty consulting services in the $250,000 range—can literally afford to live in a potential customer's lap. Because such a product allows for a $25,000 cost of sale, the company's highest-ranking executives can afford to be personally involved in the selling process, spending days, if need be, convincing and cajoling prospective customers.

The business plan should go through the same descriptive-quantitative process of explanation and justification that we have just gone through and expand on in this chapter. That is, if your company is selling a $2,000 product, you must state that you can't exceed $200 for a sales cost. You may estimate, based on market research or industry norms, that you will sell the product to one out of every five prospects. Therefore, you might indicate that you have begun lining up sales representatives to handle your company's product. You can say that you will start with representatives close to home who have an encouraging track record with your type product and gradually expand geographically.

With just such an approach, you begin to assemble a sales plan which is believable and convincing. Failure to deal clearly with such issues means that investors will be left wondering how the product or service will be sold. In such a situation, they will likely go on to the next business plan rather than wonder too long.

To help in putting the selling section of the business plan together, we have described possible selling approaches and the price ranges of products or services that match best with each:

1. *Executive selling.* This is the most luxurious approach to selling that companies can take. Senior executives essentially comprise the sales force, planning presentations, preparing proposals, and calling on potential customers.

This approach is luxurious because highly paid and highly skilled top officials are calling on customers. The fact that senior executives are devoting much time to sales work means that they are devoting less time than most other executives to such duties as managing finances, production, and the organization.

Not surprisingly, the higher the product's or service's price, the more likely it is to be a candidate for executive selling. Typically, products or services must be at least $100,000 each to qualify for an executive selling approach. Such offerings might include specialized equipment such as $500,000 CAT Scanners used as sophisticated X-ray systems in hospitals or multimillion-dollar engineering service contracts such as those sold by Stone & Webster or Bechtel, etc.

The higher the price, the more time executives can devote to selling. An executive selling expensive emission-control devices may spend days with a potential customer, assessing its needs and making adjustments in the product's design to conform with those needs.

Such products, of course, need more than aggressive executives behind them. As we will discuss later in this chapter, potential customers want to see lots of evidence of viability and support before they'll commit to paying the sorts of price tags we've been talking about to a small young company.

Exccutive selling can also be used selectively. For instance, executives might get involved with those customers who buy low-cost products in quantities that exceed $100,000. Marketing experts refer to such efforts to focus special executive selling attention on important customers as national account management.

Thus, executive selling need not be an either-or proposition. Business plans can indicate that as part of a company's selling strategy, executive selling will be targeted to customers who · meet certain buying criteria.

2. *Company sales force.* Companies which sell products or services in the $10,000 to $50,000 range can usually justify hiring their own sales force. Based on a 10% cost-of-sale allowance, the $50,000 item would allow for $5,000 of selling expense, enough to support all but the most incompetent sales force in even the toughest of sells. But it must be remembered that $50,000 items are, by virtue of their price, usually more difficult to sell than $10,000 items, so the sales force will likely have to call on more than five prospects for each sale.

The $10,000 minimum would be appropriate for most products. But if the $10,000 product turns out to be a tough sell—that is, if there's a possibility that fewer than one in five prospects will buy—it might be too borderline to justify a direct sales force. In such a situation, the $1,000 cost-of-sale allowance would be inadequate, since the amount available to call on each prospect would slip below $200.

Entrepreneurs can often anticipate the likelihood of a tough sell by examining the experiences of competitors in the industry. If there is that possibility, the business plan must address it and explain how the company's sales force would avoid it; if there is no avoiding it, then the company may have to consider the next sales approach.

3. *Sales representatives.* These are essentially independent contractors who sell the non-competing products of several companies to the same industry. Sales representatives, or sales reps, sell everything from advertising space in magazines to electronic components. Generally, products should be priced

in the range of $1,000 to $10,000 to justify such a selling approach.

Because sales reps are usually paid on a commission basis, entrepreneurs may think that they don't have to worry as much about the cost-of-sale allotment. After all, if the rep doesn't sell, he or she will have to absorb the losses, it's reasoned.

In fact, though, sales representatives aren't unlike literary agents. Just as literary agents are quite selective in the authors they will agree to represent, so are sales reps very selective in whose products they will sell. Both literary agents and sales reps want evidence of saleability; they know well the financial pitfalls of manuscripts or products that don't sell easily enough.

The sales rep has learned to cost-account the sales effort. Products that don't produce a target average income per hour are ignored or dropped. There is no free lunch.

Entrepreneurs, then, must be prepared to convince sales reps to take on their product. Company officials must convince the reps not only that the product will sell, but that it will be appropriately promoted, advertised, and serviced.

In addition to convincing the sales reps, entrepreneurs must convince potential investors that the reps will give a company's product enough attention. Potential investors worry, and rightfully so, that reps will relegate a company's product to an "oh, by the way" status far down on the presentation priority list or drop it altogether if the product isn't selling well. In investors' minds, the issue is one of control—sellers have less of it if their products are being sold by non-employees.

Thus, the business plan must offer evidence that a company has been in contact with sales reps and give some indication of the arrangements which have been worked out to ensure that the product will be well represented. We'll discuss ways to work with sales reps later in this chapter.

4. *Mass distribution.* Unless they are sold in quantity, products priced at less than $1,000 must usually be sold either off-the-shelf by wholesalers and retailers or via some form of mail order, such as catalogue or direct-mail solicitation.

In such cases, investors will want evidence of the experiences of others in selling the way you propose. For instance, if you propose to sell a newsletter by direct mail for $300 annually, you should include in your business plan the fact that response rates from such solicitations typically range from .5% to 2.5%, after allowing for subscribers who don't pay their bills.

Investors will seek evidence that those companies which propose to sell through retailers have convinced some to carry their products and that they'll be prominently displayed on the shelves. Investors know that companies attempting to get into certain businesses, such as the personal computer business, will likely discover that just getting their product out on the shelves is an extremely challenging task.

As in the case of sales reps, there's an issue of control. Outsiders essentially determine whether potential customers are appropriately exposed to a company's product.

External Support: Introducing Yourself to the Marketplace

Once you've decided how you will sell your product, you must determine who you will sell it to and how you will let potential customers know the product exists. Such tasks are part of the job of providing support to whoever is out in the field selling your product.

Determining who will buy your product would seem to be an obvious task, until you begin trying to be precise. For an example, let's use a case before the MIT Enterprise Forum of the owners of a company planning to make a computer-linked inventory control device. Their expected customers were businesses which store large quantities of inventory in warehouses—retail chains, wholesale distributors, and the health-care industry.

But one panelist was extremely concerned about who within such companies actually made the purchase decision. "There are possibly three different groups which might want to have a say about whether or not this kind of product comes in the door: the information services department, the accounting department, and the people out there in the warehouse," the panelist said. "If you aren't careful how you play that game, you can get all balled up with the various groups on who is really going to make the purchase decision. In the end, you may wind up selling to no one."

Generally speaking, the higher the price for a product or service, the more likely there are to be difficulties reaching the true purchaser. Thus, for the seller of multimillion-dollar corporate jets to go through a large company's purchase department to make its sales pitch will likely mean missing the real decision makers: senior corporate officers, advised by the corporation's pilot.

Resolving this issue is extremely important to investors and to those concerned with ultimate company success. Otherwise, young companies can easily waste follow-up steps in the selling process. That is, if a sales force is directing its efforts to the wrong individuals, there will be no sales, regardless of how talented the salespeople are.

Once entrepreneurs are aware of the true purchasers, there will sometimes be a temptation to think of the better mousetrap adage; that is, if you have one, the world will beat a path to your door. This is only half true: Sellers still need to provide buyers with a roadmap to find the better mousetrap.

The way to provide a roadmap is with publicity directed at potential buyers. Since new and young companies usually can't afford the steep rates for magazine and television advertising, such publicity is ideally obtained free by getting article writeups about new products or services in trade publications which reach potential buyers.

Such publicity serves two purposes. First, it lets prospects know of the existence of a new product or service and where to find it. Second, it lends credibility to young companies, which desperately need it. Indeed, the higher the prices for companies' products or services, the more they need credibility. In all cases, product or service brochures along with any articles describing the company and its offerings should be included in an appendix to the business plan.

The producer of a $500,000 CAT Scanner can afford executive selling and should strive mightily to identify the actual purchaser within hospitals. But once that is done, there's still the enormous task of establishing credibility in the prospect's mind. Given such a huge purchase, the customer wants to be sure the seller will still be in existence for some years down the road, to attend to the equipment's maintenance, repair, and updating.

Credibility is as much image as it is reality. A company may be nothing more than a desk in a garage, but if its product or service gets written up favorably in a publication which reaches and is respected by potential customers, the business will take on an aura of respectability and substance.

Indeed, many publications such as *Venture* and regional business magazines frequently describe new and young businesses promoting unusual real estate, consulting, and other

services. Similarly, local newspapers often review new restaurants and other food services. In the minds of potential customers, the reality will be what the article stated, not the desk
in the garage. In other words, there's no substitute for the
printed word.

Investors aren't much different from prospective customers
when it comes to the written word. Entrepreneurs who can
show evidence through articles that their products or services
are of interest to the marketplace will go a long way toward
intriguing and even exciting investors.

Articles are also much more convincing, and less costly,
than advertisements—which is a factor that entrepreneurs frequently overlook. One group of entrepreneurs proposing to
start a bank that would use automation to lower costs and pay
higher interest rates to savers than established banks included
in its business plan a provision for thousands of dollars of advertising. An outside adviser the entrepreneurs asked to examine the plan pointed out that the idea of a new type of bank
would probably be of interest to many local and national business publications, generating much credible, and free, publicity. The entrepreneurs, who hadn't realized the publicity
potential, quickly embraced the idea.

How do you get articles written about your company? Primarily by determining, first, which publications serve your
market and, second, how your message should be tailored to
serve their needs. The founders of one startup company which
was seeking to introduce a new specialized electronic component went through this process by identifying the key publications and then studying how each handled new-product
announcements. They determined that the most highly respected publication devoted an average of 124 words to individual articles about new products. So they wrote a 124-word

news release which resembled that magazine's style as closely as they could write it.

The release was published exactly as the entrepreneurs wrote it. The company received several substantial orders for the product, and it used the article to advantage in its eventual successful efforts to obtain venture capital financing.

Such publicity efforts are, of course, very time-consuming for top company officials. Such officials cannot be expected to exploit all the potentially helpful publicity opportunities available. Investors are aware of such problems and thus are favorable to the idea of young companies including in their business plans estimates for public relations expenditures.

To come up with realistic estimates, entrepreneurs should check out what other companies in their industry spend. The expenditures vary widely; companies in most areas of the personal computer industry will require a fairly substantial public relations expenditure while those in machine tools may need to allot considerably less. Entrepreneurs can sometimes find such information in the 10K reports that publicly held corporations file with the Securities and Exchange Commission or through officials of industry associations. Annual reports are not as detailed, but they can provide a useful overview.

Internal Support: The Care and Feeding of Sales Personnel

Sales support isn't simply a matter of letting the world know about your company. It's also a matter of tending to internal cost and housekeeping matters. Just as investors want to know how you will tell the marketplace you exist, they want to know that you will tend to the housekeeping matters that often determine the difference between profits and losses.

Such housekeeping matters are often referred to by investors and lenders as internal support issues—activities which
go on in companies to alter products or services and to provide sales literature and other information to the sales force.
As an example of an internal support issue, some products
must be altered or tested before they're sold to customers.
Designing and carrying out such alteration or testing can add
significantly to a product's cost—sometimes as much as an additional 5% to the cost of sale. If such costs aren't figured in to
the final price, profit margin can be significantly eroded.

Although investors aren't enamored of products or services
which require extensive alterations for each customer (as
noted in Chapter 1), they can accept the idea of some, especially if they're covered in the sales cost projections and thus
reflected in the product's price. If they are not covered and
investors have to ask about possible additional sales costs,
they may then wonder which other costs haven't been allowed
for in the business plan.

Another housekeeping issue is managing the sales force,
however it is organized. Investors want to know that it is being
effectively overseen, trained, and guided.

The more removed sellers are from a company's direct control, the more concerned investors are about supervision.
Thus, companies selling via sales reps or mass distribution
must show evidence of seller interest, expertise, and loyalty,
to allay investors' fears that products won't be sold intensely
enough. Business plans might note a sales rep's diligence in
following up sales leads of the company's product or service
or, if no previous record exists, the sales rep's record in following up the leads of a related item. Relative comparisons of
retailers and distributors in selling similar products or services
can also serve as evidence of potential seller effectiveness.

Nancy C.'s company (described in Chapter 1) came under

sharp scrutiny because of its plans to use sales reps to sell its software. "I don't get a good understanding from your plan of how much a sales rep costs, how you plan to train them in learning to use your product, what the training program will cost, and what territory each will cover," a panelist observed. "You need someone who understands sales reps to come into your company, because they are the key to increasing company sales."

Ideally, this panelist noted, the company should consider having its own sales force, especially given the fact that its product sells for between $20,000 and $30,000. The product's price would cover the costs associated with a sales force and would give the added benefit of more direct control over the sellers, the panelist indicated.

Even if a company plans to have its own sales force or rely heavily on executive selling, potential investors want evidence that entrepreneurs have considered how the salespeople will be compensated, evaluated, dispersed, and, perhaps most important, motivated. Will the salespeople be paid on a commission basis, salary plus commission, or will they be paid straight salary? Will there be bonuses, trips, prizes, or other inducements for exceptional sales performance? Will salespeople have the authority to cut prices in order to complete sales? Will evaluations be tied to factors other than total sales, such as the number of new customers added or the number of customers buying in volume? Will sales territories be determined on the basis of geography, demographics, or some other factors?

Moreover, how will the sales force be supervised? The sales manager will surely want to accompany salespeople occasionally on trips. And the sales manager will have to provide appropriate literature and qualified sales leads. This person will likely also be called on to make decisions on whether to grant price breaks or additional services that customers will constantly demand. What is equally important is how much such support will cost.

The sales section of the business plan should indicate the cost of expected trips, literature, price breaks, and additional services. Indeed, the more such questions and issues the business plan can address, the more impressed investors will be. They want to know that entrepreneurs have thought the selling process through with much care.

As a panelist remarked to Nancy C.: "You say in your plan that you are a software company. I think that what you want to say is that you are a software marketing company. That's what I want to hear, but that does not come across in your plan or in your organizational chart."

For all the questions about business-plan focus, form, and projections, investors know that there's no substitute for selling. Ventures which can vividly and clearly demonstrate that they are sales oriented will be the likeliest to receive investor backing.

IN SUMMARY

Once they have analyzed and described their potential market, entrepreneurs must explain precisely and persuasively how the venture's product or service will be sold. Possible selling approaches are as follows:

• Executive selling. Top company officials are directly involved in the selling process, usually for orders in excess of $100,000.

• Company sales force. Hired salespeople visit with prospective customers, usually with offerings in the $10,000 to $50,000 range.

• Sales representatives. Independent contractors offer the

wares of several companies, typically with items in the range of $1,000 to $10,000.

• Mass distribution. Companies with products or services of less than $1,000 most often use direct mail, retailers, catalogues, or some other large-scale merchandising.

Selling also requires two additional forms of company support:

1. Letting potential customers know the product or service exists, such as through news releases and magazine articles

2. Tending to costs of product alterations, sales literature, and other internal issues

6

Product Development and Manufacturing: Impact on Investment

THE SCENE: The offices of the Go For Broke Venture Capital Company

THE SETTING: The weekly meeting

E: Well, Mary D., what about that investor you met at the energy seminar, the one with the proposal for the small, super-economical hydroelectric power generator? With the high cost of energy and all the rivers and lakes in New England, he might be on to something.

D: He certainly talks a good game, and he very well might be on to something. Unfortunately, he's never built the device. I've checked him out and he's a good man with a fine track record of previous inventions. But . . . he needs plenty of money just to prove the feasibility—and the marketability—of his invention concept, before he can engineer it into a product. And any mistakes might be expensive: hydropower is a big-ticket business.

E: Let's pass. The risks are too high for us. I'd be very tempted if the project were further along. Linda C., how about that flavored popcorn franchising crowd you're looking into? Did you see their model store?

C: Yes. It looks beautiful and the popcorn is delicious. They've really designed the store to look futuristic, and the popcorn flavors are more authentic and fresher tasting than others I've tried. I also like the suburban shopping mall they've picked—it's *the* up-and-coming location in this area. But it's still just a prototype store. It's only been there a few months, so there's no history to it, and these people haven't demonstrated that they can sell franchises on a large scale. So both the store concept and the franchising idea need some more market research to show that there are actual customer prospects for each. As neat as the business appears, I'm still not convinced there's a real market.

E: Too bad. I'd love to get into a fast-growth franchise situation, but our group just won't put money into products which need to be scaled up from a single model to a fast-expanding chain unless the market is totally receptive, and that's tough to prove in most cases. If you can't see a market clearly, we'll drop it. Frank B., what about the software group?

B: The software works beautifully. It allows doctors to do their own billing rather than relying on service bureaus. It's a definite improvement on systems being used by service bureaus and doctors alike. And it incorporates some neat technical advances, to discourage pirating of the system. The software group has sold three systems and the customers like the stuff. The customers all told me the same thing: They're happy with the product and feel there'll be a fine market once the product becomes better known.

E: That's more like it. Let's investigate further. I'm still nervous about the market, though. Doctors are very tough customers to get at to make your pitch. Let's find out what the competition has and how this outfit plans to sell—and let's talk to a few dozen possible customers. Also, try to make sure they can produce the systems in quantity. Now, how about that new women's magazine?

A: It looks super. You may remember, this magazine is directed toward women who own their own businesses or are in corporate management—an expanding and high-income group. It's got ten thousand subscribers after its first year and has received excellent reviews in the business press. Most important, renewals are coming in at a 70% rate, which is extraordinary in that business. And that's where the real money is in magazine and newsletter publishing. They need money for the best reasons—to expand their direct mail marketing effort and reduce their production costs.

E: Let's all visit them next Tuesday. Sounds like a low-risk situation. I'd rather pay more for the stock and be able to sleep nights.

As this imaginary dialogue illustrates, investors want their money to be as productive as possible. They much prefer their funds to go directly into producing and selling the product than to support engineering, testing, market research, and other product development activities. The closer the product moves to being sold in quantity, the lower the risk and the quicker the profits are realized.

Indeed, financiers rate investment opportunities according to the overall risk and desirability of the venture. To get at that rating, they go through a process not unlike the one we will go through in this and the following two chapters.

First, in this chapter, we characterize investment opportunities as falling into one of four basic categories, or levels, according to the amount of product development which has been accomplished by the time the business plan is completed. These levels serve as important background and guideposts for writing the "Product" (or "Service") section of the business plan (Section 3 as outlined in the sample table of contents beginning on page 32). This chapter concludes by offering advice on completing the "Manufacturing" section of the business plan (Section 5 in the sample table of contents).

In Chapter 7 we present a similar set of levels for management teams. We then put the two rating approaches together with the financial analysis explained in Chapter 8 to come up with a special section that enables entrepreneurs and investors to measure the overall desirability and risk of the investment opportunity that a venture offers.

Chapters 6, 7, and 8, then, are as much about the strategy and planning that form the basis for the business plan as they are about the specifics of writing the business plan. They're about the vital business-building process which is reflected in the business plan that records and describes that process.

The four levels of product/service development, from the most to the least desirable, are as follows:

Level 4: A Going Concern

In this venture, the product or service has not only been developed, but it is being produced and sold to customers who are happy with it. The customers are willing to extol the product and its long-term prospects in the industry to inquiring investors, who should be encouraged—even physically transported—to see the product being used.

The Level 4 venture requires capital to broaden marketing and sales efforts—to scout out new customer segments and expand the sales force. The capital may also be needed to increase manufacturing capacity to take advantage of economies of scale and thus improve the prospects for substantial cash flow, profits, and growth. Under these conditions, the founders can value their company highly, based upon projections which have a clear ring of credibility to them.

On those occasions when solid Level 4 ventures appear at the MIT Enterprise Forum, they invariably stir up lots of interest. In one instance a few years ago, Joseph B., the president of a company which had developed automatic control systems to make more efficient the operation of machine tools, came armed with a concise and clearly written business plan, slides of his product performing at a happy customer's plant, and a healthy backlog of orders. He needed investment funds, he explained in his presentation, to expand his manufacturing capacity to fill the order backlog and be prepared to generate an expected substantial growth in future orders.

The panelists were clearly impressed with his business plan, based on their complimentary remarks and relatively minor suggestions for changes in the plan. When the time came for audience questions and comments, an individual who identified himself as a partner in a venture capital firm requested that Joseph B. appear at the venture capitalist firm's offices at eleven o'clock the next morning! Joseph B.'s company obtained funding within three weeks.

We should add, though, that being a Level 4 company doesn't guarantee obtaining investment funds. After all, there are lots of going businesses turning out perfectly fine products which aren't investment candidates because they haven't shown necessary growth prospects. Suitable Level 4 candidates must be able to assemble an attractive business plan which demonstrates that the company has the growth potential that investors seek.

Founders must not lose sight of the fact that investors are seeking compound rates of capital appreciation of 35% to 60% annually; for a Level 4 venture, rates closer to the 35% end of the scale are likelier to be acceptable than for less-developed businesses. Many Level 4 ventures will have difficulty demonstrating even the 35% capital growth rate, though.

Go For Broke Venture Capital Company notwithstanding, not all investors prefer Level 4 candidates. Although venture capital firms have traditionally sought out such companies, investors are increasingly receptive to more embryonic opportunities, which have the potential of achieving greater capital appreciation at a lower investment cost.

Level 3: Ready to Go

Companies at this stage have completed development and engineering of their product or service, so that it is ready for aggressive marketing and sales efforts. That is, a real product or service exists. It can be tested and analyzed by experts whom potential investors employ or hire.

When a group of entrepreneurs put together a business plan seeking to raise funds for a mail-order business which would use a graphically appealing catalogue to sell specialty ethnic foods, potential investors asked for a sample catalogue. The company didn't have one, but they decided that a two-month and $3,000 investment in making a sample catalogue was necessary to convince investors the entrepreneurs were serious. The sample catalogue that resulted not only encouraged investors to take a much closer look at backing the new business, but it provided the entrepreneurs with valuable experience in evaluating their final product.

Certainly the fact that a workable production-ready product exists is extremely important and in many cases will attract the interest of investors who are somewhat more risk-oriented than those who snap at Level 4 opportunities. Level 3 investors know that a given amount of investment will usually purchase a larger piece of the company than in a Level 4 situation, and they can be influenced to take the plunge if they have solid evidence of substantial market interest.

On the negative side, the product likely hasn't been tried or installed in more than a few installations to demonstrate its value and probable widescale acceptance. Indeed, there may not even be any permanent installations; the prototype may just have been loaned out to a few potential customers. Ease of production is still an unknown quantity.

Investors know that a substantial difference exists in terms of risk between the Level 4 and Level 3 situations. The difference is that, despite the *evidence* of market interest and that the product can be produced in quantity, there's no *guarantee* of either. Around Route 128, investors still talk about the classic case illustrating that point—that of Viatron Computer Systems Corp.

Viatron made a grand entrance onto the computer scene in the late 1960s and early 1970s by obtaining investor and public funds to produce and market a minicomputer for rental to customers at an extremely low monthly rate. The company appeared to be a sure winner, as the $35 million it raised in the public markets would seem to attest.

For all the hoopla, though, Viatron was essentially a Level 3 company. The company had received many orders for the computer, but it had only produced a very few models of the product. Unfortunately, when the company tried to produce the computer in quantity, it encountered problems.

Viatron was able to offer a low price on the computer because it made use of a new inexpensive semiconductor chip. The chip had never been produced in quantity before and, when Viatron started assembling its computers, the supplier of the chip ran into production problems. That delayed shipment of Viatron's computers.

As customers began cancelling orders, Viatron built new production capacity in a desperate attempt to make the chip itself. The tactic failed, and Viatron was left holding the bag of a huge production capacity, which quickly became an unjustified expense. In 1970, the company lost more than $30 million on sales of just $2.5 million, and it subsequently went bankrupt and was liquidated.

The Boston-area venture capital community has never forgotten the example of Viatron. Its sad history says to venture capitalists that the "due diligence" process must take into account every detail to ensure that such seemingly minor problems as the semiconductor production difficulty don't create last-minute surprises—and debacles. (It is a lot like, "For want of a nail, the shoe was lost; for want of a shoe, the horse was lost; for want of the horse, the battle was lost; and the kingdom was lost.")

Many Level 3 situations go on to become major successes. Founders and investors must simply make sure that the plans rest on a solid foundation. Also, entrepreneurs must expect to give up a larger share of their companies to the investors than in the case of a Level 4 situation.

Level 2: Almost There

Companies at this stage have built a product prototype, which works successfully, but it isn't yet ready for marketing and production because it still requires additional evaluation and engineering. The product also requires customer testing to verify user benefit and the appropriateness of the package and various features which have been designed into the pre-production model. After all production engineering is completed and appropriate adjustments made, there will have to be tooling and designing of production facilities. In addition, marketing and sales have to be developed before a real business is possible.

Thus, at least some part—and probably a substantial part—of any investment funds will need to be spent on completing such product and marketing development tasks. And even before that, potential investors will have to put in an inordinate amount of time and energy investigating whether the product can indeed be engineered for production without major modifications and whether the production design is appropriate to the needs and requirements of prospective users. After all that investigation, of course, there is no guarantee, from the investors' perspective, that everything will come together as hoped.

As a consequence of such uncertainty, investors in Level 2 situations expect a larger share than for Level 3 or 4 situations of any companies in which they invest—that is, provided a particular Level 2 company can indeed attract an investor.

Entrepreneurs who appear at the MIT Enterprise Forum with their product development at the Level 2 stage are frequently advised to tighten their belts and somehow beg, borrow, or steal the money they need to move themselves up to a Level 3 situation. Such interim assistance can be provided in any number of ways, ranging from borrowing from relatives to obtaining a government research contract to getting potential customers to pay up-front for the product at a discount price.

Indeed, two members of the MIT Enterprise Forum executive committee had a company at this stage and took just such an approach. Their company had produced a model of a machine which transforms written text into spoken words, for use by blind and visually handicapped individuals as well as in office automation. But the product needed further development and engineering to iron out technical problems and achieve the results expected by the inventors.

The founders obtained a federal research and development contract to complete the development and engineering. That enabled the company to place their machines in many libraries throughout the United States for use by the blind.

It also enabled the company to upgrade the machine into office equipment capable of "reading" incoming correspondence and documents and transferring them directly into computer memory. This capability saves users filing and storage space and makes any letter or document instantly accessible to others in an office.

That government contract essentially took the company from Level 2 to Level 3, where it obtained investment funds. The company eventually succeeded and was sold to a major corporation, where it is now an important subsidiary.

The only exceptions to the negative effects of being at Level 2 are usually those entrepreneurs with a significant record of previous successes. A previous winning track record can induce investors to "take a flier," so to speak. Barring that track record, Level 2 companies will find investment funds difficult to come by.

Level 1: A Great Idea, But . . .

Great ideas, investors know, are ten cents for twelve. It may even be possible to put together a dummy model in a laboratory or shop and write a perfectly coherent business plan based on the concept. But to get investors to put money up for a Level 1 product requires that either of two conditions are met.

One possibility is that the founders be proven magicians or

geniuses, who can be depended on to succeed at almost anything they feel like doing. Such individuals do exist, but they're extremely rare, and most mortals simply don't qualify.

The other possibility is an idea which is such an obvious winner that investors believe it simply can't fail. Some of the genetic engineering companies which sprang up in the early 1980s, backed by venture capital firms, were the outcomes of such thinking. Actual products were years into the future, investors knew, but there was no question that, when finally produced, the products—including prevention, treatment, or cure for diseases ranging from diabetes to certain cancers—would be extremely marketable.

For most good ideas, though, the advice investors give to entrepreneurs is to somehow produce something tangible. In one case, founders of a company appeared at an MIT Enterprise Forum session seeking several hundred thousand dollars to make a prototype of a computerized walkie-talkie inventory control system for warehousing.

The walkie-talkie would have a complete punch pad and voice communication capability for input. Workers would carry the control system from place to place and punch in or dictate the requisite information corresponding to the actual inventory, product identification numbers, and other pertinent information leading to automatic reordering of needed items for inventory.

The idea was obviously workable, the panelists agreed. And although the founders planned to engineer some proprietary developments into the product, it was clear they weren't so futuristic as to make production of the product especially difficult.

Because the product wasn't actually built and operating, panelists were concerned about the degree of compatibility between the proposed new system and the existing computer systems many companies already had in place in their warehouses. The panelists also wondered how much customizing would need to be done to adapt the product to the needs of each customer.

Despite the fact that the entrepreneurs had done an admirable amount of marketing research, they couldn't give totally convincing answers to such questions because the product wasn't far enough along in its development to have allowed for complete investigation of such issues.

Thus, although it was obvious the idea would work, it was also obvious to panelists that much investment funding would be consumed by product development before one dime of cash flow could be realized. In addition, panelists noted, any potential investors would likely want a substantial majority of the company, perhaps with an option to sell some of the ownership back to the founders after the product was being manufactured and positive cash flow had been achieved.

The overall feeling, as expressed by one panelist, was that the entrepreneurs should "go back and sharpen up your act"—in other words, get farther down the product development path. That might entail borrowing funds from friends or relatives so as to somehow have a product that could be shown to investors and potential customers.

Some fledgling Level 1 businesses can solicit development contracts from either government or private industry to aid in product development. For instance, the National Science Foundation makes research grants of $50,000 to inventors and others for investigation and research of promising ideas. Recipients who make suitable progress can then obtain follow-up grants of up to $500,000 to complete development of the product and make it ready for selling.

Not surprisingly, competition for such grants is extremely keen. No proposal may be more than twenty pages long, and awards are given twice yearly to those businesses which convincingly demonstrate that the idea will lead to product commercialization sometime in the not-too-distant future. The entrepreneurs aren't required to give up either equity or proprietary rights to the government in exchange for the funds, either. Grants are meant to stimulate development of new technology and viable businesses.

Recent federal legislation makes it easier for young companies to obtain research funding from any of dozens of other government agencies to transform a product from the idea stage to commercialization. These include the Department of Defense, the Environmental Protection Agency, the National Institutes of Health, and others. This support can come in the form either of research or other development funds leading to a product the agency can purchase.

Information about seeking out such government support is available from the Small Business Administration's Office of Advocacy, 1441 L St. NW, Washington, DC 20416.

Alternatively, private industry will sometimes provide development funds and a profit-sharing or royalty arrangement in return for commitments to joint ventures or rights to market the developed product. Many companies have also accomplished their product development tasks by obtaining private consulting or development contracts from interested users or producers.

In one case, entrepreneurs obtained a consulting contract from a major textile firm to develop an instrument that measured certain properties of textile and paper fibers. The textile company paid for all the product development in return for about two years of lead time before the product was sold to competitors. In addition, the founders were required to pay royalties to the textile company until it had received three times its original investment. If that seems expensive, consider that when the whole process was complete, the founders still owned their entire company.

More recently, Softword Systems Inc., producer of the popular Multimate word processing software, accomplished its product development under contract from a major insurance company. The "sponsor" wanted a word processing program for use on its IBM Personal Computers that would emulate its existing Wang word processors. When Softword Systems was finished developing the system under contract, it had a product which transformed the consulting firm into a multimillion-dollar producer of microcomputer software.

Unfortunately, information about corporations offering such contracts isn't available from a single source; entrepreneurs must establish contacts within their industry to inform them about possible consulting opportunities.

Entrepreneurs can also consider R&D Limited Partnerships and Subchapter S corporations—both of which offer high-tax-bracket individuals substantial tax writeoffs in return for investing. (Subchapter S corporations channel ventures' early losses directly to investors' personal income tax statements.) These devices require the advice and assistance of experienced accountants. Of course, those entrepreneurs with a previous track record will find it easiest to attract such development funds.

Finally, what about all those entrepreneurs we read or hear about who receive investment funds based on some drawings they put on damp cocktail napkins or the back of an envelope? Those cases do occur, but careful examination of each case shows that circumstances existed to indicate clearly that the proposal was a likely winner. The entrepreneurs probably had brilliant track records and had done some convincing market analysis; in addition, the idea undoubtedly was an obvious low risk.

There's no getting around the fact that in most circumstances Level 4 opportunities have an advantage over Level 3 situations, which are preferable to Level 2, and so on.

Turning Out the Product

The farther along the product development process is, the easier it is to be specific and convincing about issues which must be addressed in the manufacturing section of the business plan. Among the key production issues are the following:

1. How much research and development (R&D), if any, is required before the product can be engineered for manufacturing? The business plan must provide clear estimates of the material, time required, and other costs of any such efforts. These costs will include essentially all the payroll and overhead necessary to run the company until the R&D is completed.

2. Once the R&D is completed, how much engineering is required to ready the product for manufacturing in quantity? That is, what sorts of adjustments must be made in design and tooling, and how much will these adjustments cost in manpower, materials, and time? Furthermore, what sorts of engineering will be necessary as continuing sources of support for manufacturing and sales? In some cases, minor adjustments must be made to allow for variations in product features. In other cases, major customizing work must be done from one order to another. Products designed to be sold "off the shelf" usually require the least amount of ongoing engineering.

3. What kind of laboratory for ongoing testing of product performance is needed and how much will its establishment and maintenance cost? The more custom, or applications, engineering that must be done, the more elaborate a laboratory

facility will be required. The applications laboratory typically serves to help in product development and sales promotion These functions should be differentiated according to their costs.

4. How will quality control be maintained? Many young companies get so caught up in the excitement of their product that they neglect quality control as if it were an unimportant detail. Poor quality control, though, leads to frustration for customers and unnecessarily high warranty and replacement costs for producers. Products are returned for repair or replacement—at a high cost in dollars and goodwill. Indeed, it's much cheaper to produce high-quality products than shoddy products.

In overlooking quality control, entrepreneurs are often caught off-guard when financial problems result. Officials of a semiconductor manufacturer, which has $2.5 million annual sales and no profits, made a presentation at an MIT Enterprise Forum session. The founders were seeking expansion capital in the belief that further sales growth was necessary to generate those elusive profits.

Under questioning by a panelist, a company official disclosed that the company was shipping only 35% of the products it produced. In other words, 65% of all production consisted of rejects! After further questioning, the official disclosed that no one had responsibility for dealing with quality control problems in the manufacturing process.

The panelists were unanimous in advising the presenters that they would likely encounter resistance in raising funds for a company that was not only unprofitable, but showed no promise of becoming profitable. Panelists advised the entrepreneurs that cutting their rejection rate in half—which would still be below industry standards—would provide enough profit so that the company wouldn't even need to seek additional investment funds.

Indeed, quality control is an intrinsic cost of manufacturing and must be dealt with squarely in the business plan. Entrepreneurs should list costs and benefits associated with quality control. Investors will be impressed with the maturity and sophistication of founders who address this important issue.

5. How will the product be manufactured and how much will manufacturing costs be? The manufacturing issue should be dealt with five years into the future, since it will change as the company matures. It may be that during the first two years, the product will be assembled from components furnished by others and then in the next three years partly manufactured in-house from its own and outsiders' components. The costs and reasoning behind the evolution of the manufacturing process should be itemized and discussed in the business plan.

Investors usually prefer, at least during a company's early years, that more funds be concentrated on selling the product and less on the "bricks and mortar" associated with producing the product. Thus, entrepreneurs are usually better off early on to subcontract for components and processes than to invest in the facilities for handling such production tasks in-house.

Businesses especially dependent on certain raw materials should list them and demonstrate the existence of second sources, in case bottlenecks develop which could strangle production. Similarly, the business plan should indicate if certain locations are preferred for production because of their proximity to raw materials or markets. Highly detailed evaluations can be included in the second volume of the business plan to avoid bogging down the main volume with excess verbiage.

The make-buy decision seems to be an especially thorny one

for many fledgling businesses. The founders of one company appearing at the MIT Enterprise Forum had expended much of its financial resources assembling its own facilities for producing printed circuit boards. Their rationale was twofold: first, the company wouldn't have to pay subcontractor price markups and, second, it could control its own production quantity and quality.

Although those were logical arguments, the founders ignored the fact that the plant sat idle 75% of the time because sales didn't yet justify the expensive facility. To avoid losses on the facility, management was forced to spend much of its valuable time locating subcontracting business it could do for other companies to cover the overhead. This was a clear waste of administrative energy, and it distracted attention from obtaining new business.

Panelists advised the officials to shut down the production facility and find subcontractors for the company's product. Taking these steps, the panelists argued, would be painful but would end the serious bleeding of important company resources.

Entrepreneurs must calculate rather than guess at the impact of producing items in-house as opposed to farming them out. Although the temptation is to have as much control of the process as possible by bringing production in-house, entrepreneurs should keep in mind that many companies make fortunes without ever manufacturing anything themselves. Clothing and electronic companies, for instance, commonly subcontract the manufacturing of their products and essentially assume the role of product marketers. Each case must be presented on its own merits and argued carefully in the business plan.

IN SUMMARY

Explaining a company's product and manufacturing process is more a matter of action than of writing. The further along the product is in the development process and the more definite the manufacturing situation is, the more convincing the business plan will be, simply because it will be describing what has occurred rather than what is expected to occur. The product development process can be broken down into four levels:

• Level 4—a completed product which has been sold to satisfied customers
• Level 3—a completed product which hasn't yet been produced in significant quantity
• Level 2—a product prototype which requires additional evaluation and engineering
• Level 1—an impressive product idea which hasn't yet been developed to the prototype stage

The higher the level of product development, the more specific information that can be offered about such particulars of the manufacturing process as research and development, engineering, ongoing testing, and quality control.

7

What's the Management Team Like?

There are two ways to bet on horse races. First, one can compare the records of the horses in the field. Clearly, a good horse with a proven record will attract many bettors, which is reflected in the low odds accorded a favorite.

A second approach—the one favored by some race track aficionados—is to bet on a jockey with a winning record who is riding a horse without much of a record. Bettors know that a skilled jockey can often bring a less-than-perfect horse home a winner.

Professional investors are much like seasoned horse-race bettors in seeking out winners. Venture capitalists are fond of saying that, given the choice between a first-rate product being produced by second-rate managers and a mediocre product produced by top-notch managers, they'd prefer the latter. That is, people have priority over products, or horses.

This chapter provides important background for completing the "Management Team" portion of the business plan (part of the description of "The Company," Section 1, in our sample table of contents, which begins on page 32.) Each team member's background and qualifications should be summarized in two or three paragraphs in this portion of the plan; full-page biographical sketches or résumés of each member should then be included as an appendix to the plan.

This chapter also presents additional criteria to enable entrepreneurs and investors to evaluate the attractiveness of ventures for investment. These criteria are used—together with criteria developed in Chapters 6 and 8—to develop the Rich-Gumpert method for rating investments, which follows Chapter 8.

What do investors mean when they say they want the best people? And how can the business plan assure them of the entrepreneurs' qualifications? One way to begin answering these questions is to consider what investors don't want.

One-Man Bands Needn't Apply

When investors say they want top managers, there is a big emphasis on the plural. Investors don't care for companies founded and operated by a single entrepreneur—no matter how savvy a manager that individual might be.

That became very clear when the proprietor of a three-year-old company that produced printed circuit boards appeared before an MIT Enterprise Forum session. He wanted advice, he told the panelists, on how he could get his sales out of the $50,000 to $100,000 range, where they seemed to be stuck, and closer to the multimillion-dollar range of some of his competitors.

"Who is the chief executive officer?" a panelist asked.

"I am," the entrepreneur answered.

"Who is the chief financial officer?"

"I am."

"Who is head of engineering?"

"I am."

"Who is the sales manager?"

"I am."

"How much of your time do you devote to sales?" the same panelist asked.

"About 10%," came the answer.

To which the panelist responded, "If you had someone putting 100% of their time into sales, it's almost certain your company's revenues could increase to between $500,000 and $1 million."

The owner took the panelist's advice, and his company has since begun to live up to its promise.

In another case that came before the MIT Enterprise Forum, the founder of an electric-motor manufacturing business complained that he was working too hard running the company, which had grown to $2 million annual sales. He had other managers, but they were all at a much lower level than the founder in terms of pay and responsibility; they also didn't own any stock in the company.

The entrepreneur clearly had trouble giving up control of any sort—be it responsibility or ownership—to others. One panelist suggested that the entrepreneur consider involving himself in some outside activities, such as an industry trade association, to break his iron grip on the business.

He became involved in a trade association and, in doing so, hired some key executives, to whom he delegated authority and sold stock in the company. The company's growth rate improved, and the entrepreneur's work load eased.

As these examples suggest, one-man bands tend to run into limitations by virtue of the fact that a single individual can only accomplish so much in a twenty-four-hour day. In the view of investors, the entrepreneur who tries to be all things to all people winds up being of diminished worth overall.

To investors, the antidote to the one-man-band syndrome is the management team. In their view, the management team—

usually consisting of three to six executives—reduces risks associated with the one-man band in two key areas. First, a management team ensures that all important management jobs—production, sales, and finance, among others—will be tended to. Second, a team ensures that the business can survive the loss of a key person to such vagaries as illness, accident, or recruitment by a competitor.

The Supreme Challenge

Putting a winning team together, as any sports fan knows, is no easy task. A winning baseball, basketball, or hockey team needs to be skilled, balanced, driven, and harmonious. An inexperienced shortstop, a lackadaisical guard, or a hot-dog left wing can prevent an otherwise effective team from getting to the top.

So it is with smaller companies. More often than not, they are prevented from performing to their true potential because of difficulties among the team members. One recent survey of 170 businesses which were members of the Smaller Business Association of New England (SBANE) and which had started with teams found that, by the time of the survey, more than two-thirds of the partnerships had broken up. About 60% of those breakups were because of changing interests or interpersonal conflict among the team members.

Interests often change because the partners in a business don't have a clear understanding ahead of time of what they want their companies to be when they grow up. If one partner wants a cash cow and another a potentially large corporation, then interests are likely at some point to diverge. Interpersonal conflicts most often occur over management tasks and money; one partner may feel that another isn't working hard enough or skillfully enough, or else partners may argue over the fairness of salaries and ownership stakes.

At the same time, limited research on the subject of management teams suggests that businesses managed by two or more principals with complementary business skills often provide for the greatest growth potential. A survey in 1983 by *Inc.* magazine of the one hundred fastest-growing public companies found that two-thirds of their founders had at least one partner, three-fourths of whom were still in the business.

As this research and our own experience suggest, then, assembling a winning management team is at once one of the most important and most difficult tasks facing a young venture. Potential investors look at the management team with the same critical gaze they use to assess the marketing, sales, and product projections.

Thus, the management team should be described, at least briefly, in the executive summary, as well as within the plan's first section, which describes the company, and via the biographical sketches or résumés attached to the end of the plan. At each point, the plan should highlight the team members' past experience and skills likeliest to contribute to the venture at hand. Moreover, the plan should emphasize how the team members' individual specialties will complement each other to the advantage of the company. These issues are dealt with in greater detail in this chapter's next section.

Failure to provide enough detail will raise eyebrows among potential investors, as it did at an MIT Enterprise Forum session at which a principal of a photovoltaics product company spent much time extolling the young company's special technology. "You need to say more about your management team," an investor in the audience observed. "Remember, you are starting a business and the product is only the entry into the business. The people are at least equally important."

Among the questions confronting fledgling businesses seeking to put together a winning team are the following:

- How do investors evaluate management teams?
- How can cash-poor young businesses fill key slots?
- How can top managers most effectively be motivated and discouraged from jumping ship to start their own companies?

The Right Stuff

Management teams ideally consist of people in charge of the key executive areas—marketing, sales, operations, finances, manufacturing, and engineering. These are the bases which should be covered with people of the highest caliber, experience, and training.

Too often, though, individuals choosing business partners go through a process not unlike the one they follow when they choose companions for lunch or a party. That is, they tend to get together in business with people who are very much like themselves. Computer engineers get together with other computer engineers; chemists seek out other chemists, and so on and so forth.

Most commonly, they get together to produce a particular product or service that one of the individuals thought up or that they had some experience working on together while employed by a large corporation. How they got together isn't as important as the fact that teams frequently consist of people with similar backgrounds and skills. Most often, the teams are product oriented rather than marketing or financially oriented. That is, they focus too heavily on the technicalities of their product or service rather than on how it will be sold and financed.

Such teams frequently approach MIT Enterprise Forum executive committee members and appear at Enterprise Forum sessions in search of investor funds. One such team approached a member of the executive committee seeking backing for a service that would collect and sell business data. Unfortunately, the business plan was so wrapped up in describing the nature of the data and how it would be assembled that little attention was given to the qualifications of the team members along with other issues as user benefit and market size.

When the executive committee member inquired into the management team's qualifications, it turned out that none of the team members were marketing or sales experts. The business finally attracted limited backing in a joint venture arrangement with a larger company, but it floundered for several years afterward.

Another such team, which appeared at an Enterprise Forum session, included a group of four engineers specializing in laser and fiber-optics technology; their company had specialized for three years in doing government- and industry-sponsored research-and-development projects and sought $2 million of funding to make the transition to producing its own products.

One of the engineers described in considerable detail the products the venture had on the drawing boards. They included lasers that would make certain instruments much more precise in their measurement abilities and a fiber-optics device that would be an improvement on existing devices for measuring electrical power.

The comments of one panelist were typical of the reactions: "I just love the physics behind your product line. The products are very impressive." But, he noted, he was bothered by the fact that all the principals in the company had similar backgrounds. In particular, he thought the venture needed a marketing executive with a high-technology background, to decide which products the company should focus its development and selling efforts on.

A professional investor in the audience seconded that opinion. "You seem top-heavy in engineers. You need some people who know how to build companies based on new technology—a financial executive, a hard-nosed production man, and so forth."

As this example makes clear, investors don't just want to see a group of two or more people starting a business. Investors also want to see evidence that the team members possess a variety of management skills. In addition to product development experts, there must be marketing and financial experts.

Investors seek one additional, more intangible, quality in evaluating management teams. For want of a better term, we might refer to it as experience, stability, or maturity.

The need for this quality was made strikingly apparent when the three founders of a five-month-old venture made a presentation before the MIT Enterprise Forum. The fledgling business seemed to have much going for it. It had a glamorous product—an advance in office automation that enabled people to leave voice messages and dictation on personal computers from outside their offices. In five months, the company had already developed a prototype that it demonstrated at the Enterprise Forum meeting. The business plan was well organized and written. The venture also had a seemingly well-balanced management team. All three founders had worked for a large and respected high-technology company. Two had graduated from MIT and the third had received an MBA from Harvard Business School.

Nonetheless, their initial efforts to obtain $300,000 of financing from venture capitalists had been unproductive. The reason offered, said one of the principals, with a hurt expression, was that the management team was too young.

A panelist tried to explain the venture capitalists' reasoning. "You guys are all in your twenties, so the venture capitalists see you as young. To them, young translates to high risk. So you've got to figure out a way to reduce that risk."

The panelist offered two possible ways of accomplishing that. One was to add an older, experienced executive to the team, "someone with just a touch of gray at the temples." The other was for the existing team members to prove themselves further, preferably by getting some orders for their product, with up-front payments that would enable the company to fill the orders.

Investors ideally want a team comprised of people who have been through the experience of developing a product or service and taking it to market. The members can have obtained this experience starting a company or working in a large company.

Investors' reasoning is fairly simple. They figure, for one thing, that those who have succeeded before are likeliest to succeed again. They also want reassurance that the management team not only has the required assortment of skills but the needed toughness, or true grit, necessary to carry the business through the inevitable crises all young companies encounter. Putting such an assortment of skill and experience together is no easy task for most fledgling businesses.

Finding and Attracting the Right People

Actually assembling a management team that will impress investors is one of the most difficult, and sensitive, tasks facing the young business. How it carries out that task will likely affect both the venture's likelihood of attracting capital and its chances of ultimate success.

What makes the task so challenging is the special nature of the fledgling business. It is typically cash-poor, and its prospects for eventual success are quite uncertain. Under those circumstances, it's impossible to recruit key managers the way established companies do it—by offering an attractive package of pay and benefits.

The only real incentive the new business can offer to prospective team members is the possibility, at some time in the future, of getting rich. The new business offers that incentive in the form of stock in the company. That's a not insignificant incentive, but it's an incentive that is difficult to quantify. After all, how real is the possibility of realizing sizeable returns? And approximately when in the future will the returns be realized? And how rich is rich?

And regardless of how much stock team members receive, they still must be able to put food on the table. A young company which expects a manager to join it full-time needs to be able to pay that person a living wage.

Entrepreneurs seeking to put together a winning team, then, must confront two key issues as they go about the recruitment task. First, they must decide how much stock to offer to team members. Second, they must figure out how they're going to compensate the members prior to receiving large-scale financing.

No easy answer exists for either issue. Because company stock is the only real currency entrepreneurs have, they all too often give more of it away early in the company's history than they should. They tend not to realize their error until they are seeking to raise capital and investors lay claim to between 30% and 70% of the company in exchange for the needed funds.

If each of three partners figured to own 25% of a company, with 25% left over for investors, and suddenly investors are insisting on 35% of the company, that 25% stake per partner shrinks to 15%. And if the investors insist as a precondition to investing that a fourth team member with some special expertise be added to the company, then the percentage ownership will likely shrink further, since the new member will no doubt insist on receiving stock to join a fledgling company; the investors will support that idea to ensure continuity and loyalty.

No matter how the stock pie is divided, there's still no provision for paying team members. The founding partners often try to get by on a combination of savings and part-time work. But if they need another partner with some special experience, they quickly realize that they can't do much for that person in terms of salary.

The situation of a founding team of two or three members needing another one or two members is not uncommon. As noted previously, the founding entrepreneurs tend to have similar skills—they may be all engineers or all sales experts— and they're in need of managers with complementary skills.

Panelists at the MIT Enterprise Forum encourage entrepreneurs in such situations to be imaginative. When a two-man team—one person with financial skills and the other with technical skills—running a struggling electronics company stated at an MIT Enterprise Forum session that they couldn't afford to hire an obviously badly needed sales manager, a panelist responded:

"You can't afford *not* to have a sales manager. You've got to be creative in how you approach the situation. One way to go about it is to find a person with the sales management experience you need and sell that person stock in your company at a favorable price (if you can first sell the salesman on the company). Then use the money that person puts in to pay his or her salary. You can offer additional stock incentives as a bonus on sales to make it worthwhile to that individual to work hard and stay on with the company."

Although such an answer isn't specific about such things as the amount of stock to be handed out or sold to team members, it makes an important point: There are no hard and fast rules insofar as investors are concerned about how best to put together the management team. Indeed, investors recognize the importance of flexibility, within certain limits. They are willing to seriously consider business plans which don't name each member of the management team or which acknowledge that one or two slots remain to be filled.

From the investor perspective, management teams can be rated as falling into one of four categories, or levels, from most to least preferable, as follows:

Level 4: All members of the team are identified and fully committed. This is the ideal situation. The management team is on board and working. The business plan names all members, indicates their salaries and stock ownership, and describes their relevant business experience in a paragraph or so for each person. In addition, the business plan includes as an appendix a one-page biographical sketch or résumé of each partner. And all team members have a good record of training and experience.

Level 3: All members of the team are identified, but not everyone is on board. It may be that two founders are working at the company full-time, but a third member (and possibly a fourth) who was recruited after the founding for his or her special skills is waiting for the financing to be completed before leaving an existing job. The third (and possibly fourth) member has reached an understanding about salary and stock in the new company. As in the previous situation, the team members, salaries and stock ownership, relevant experience, and résumés should be included in the business plan. There's always the danger that, despite an earlier commitment, the identified prospective management-team members will decline to join. This possibility worries investors.

Level 2: One or more members of the team are not identified and are not yet with the company. The situation may be the same as that just described, except that the third and fourth members of the team have not been found and identified.

In such a circumstance, the business plan can describe the slots for the third and fourth persons in terms of experience, salary and stock ownership, and desired background. The missing people will have to be recruited, which can be a problem, rendering a Level 2 management team less desirable.

Level 1: The one-man band. There is one founder, with no one else identified. This type of situation is usually unacceptable to investors. The one exception is the founder with an outstanding previous track record, who has brought several products from conception through to successful and profitable manufacturing and marketing. In that case, venture capitalists or other investors may get involved in helping fill in the missing team links.

Entrepreneurs should be aware that each of these management team levels has an important cost and benefit. From the viewpoint of investors, these four levels are arranged in order of decreasing preference and increasing risk. That is, the situations become progressively less desirable, because the assurance of a full team being assembled decreases in each circumstance. As we noted, in the Level 3 situation, the team member committed to joining the new company after it receives financing could receive an important promotion in his or her old job and decide at some point during negotiations over financing, or even after financing has been obtained, not to join the venture.

In return for taking on what they perceive as increasing risk, investors will demand a larger amount of equity for their investment. Thus, a company which might have gotten away with selling a 40% stake in a Level 4 circumstance, with a full management team on hand and identified, might have to give up a 50% to 60% stake as a Level 2 group, in which the investors have to recruit team members.

That helps explain why two principals of a pension management consulting firm seeking funding to develop and market special software for pension-fund managers passed around a questionnaire at an MIT Enterprise Forum session seeking names of possible marketing executives. The two realized both that they needed someone with marketing skills to complement their own technical skills and also that they'd give up less of their company with such a person on board. Panelists and audience members were also impressed with the entrepreneurs' aggressiveness in seeking to fill the slot.

On the other hand, the later in the venture creation process new team members are recruited, the less they can usually demand in terms of company ownership. Thus, a team member who joins the company at its founding might reasonably expect between 15% and 20% of the company, while a key person who agrees to come on board once the financing is being negotiated may only receive between 5% and 10% of ownership.

Overall, though, entrepreneurs should be looking toward satisfying investor requirements for a complete team rather than seeking to minimize the amount of stock being allocated by delaying recruitment of all members of the team. After all, the amount of stock that is saved by delaying recruitment isn't worth anything in the long run without investor support.

Motivating the Teammates

Entrepreneurs may figure that once they have obtained financing, they have protection in the event some teammates jump ship. That is, the founders now have the cash to replace anyone who leaves.

Fortunately for the business, investors won't take such a short-sighted view of the situation. Nor should entrepreneurs. Teammates departing, stock in hand, shortly after the venture is financed, not only weakens the developing company, but it often creates new competitors, since managers tend to leave to start their own businesses.

Entrepreneurs should take three steps to reassure investors that key members of the management team will remain with the company for at least a few years into its development:

1. *Use golden handcuffs.* It's important for founders who agree to give stock to key managers in return for joining a fledgling company not to grant all the stock up-front. Rather, the stock should be made available gradually, over a period of four or five years.

Thus, if a key manager joins a new company with the understanding that she or he will receive approximately 10% ownership, 2% of the stock might be made available up-front, with 2% at the end of each year of employment, so that the manager wouldn't get all 10% until after four years of employment. In addition to discouraging key employees from jumping ship, such an arrangement encourages them to work hard to increase the value of their future stock.

Such stock can be made available at nominal cost by segregating at the company's founding special shares known as "founders' stock" from other stock to be sold to investors. These shares might be available at one cent to five cents a share to key members of the management team. It's most important for attracting and keeping new members of the team other than founders, though, since the original one, two, or three people in a business typically put some of their own money into the company and are thus less inclined to walk away from their "baby."

Under these conditions, the company requires a buy-back agreement with the employee to purchase back all of the stock at the employee's cost if the employee leaves before a year is up; then 80%, 60%, 40%, and 20% if the person departs in two, three, four, or five years. This allows for "vesting" similar to a stock option plan.

2. *Compensate everyone in the same way.* Because a young venture's stock is in most cases virtually illiquid during its first few years, team members are sometimes tempted to try to work out special deals for themselves to increase their salaries. The sales executive wants some kind of bonus for each repeat customer or the manufacturing executive wants a bonus for extra sales resulting from beating the timetable for producing the product.

In one case that came before the MIT Enterprise Forum, the president and chief engineer of a company seeking funds to produce and market an auto-theft-prevention device had decided they deserved special compensation as inventors of the device. They noted in the business plan their provision for a special 10% royalty from sales for themselves as inventors of the product. Other members of the management team wouldn't share in the proceeds.

A venture capitalist on the panel was extremely disapproving of the arrangement: "Our firm insists that everyone be paid in the same way. If there is to be some additional income based on company performance, it should be in the form of a profit-sharing program everyone shares in. If some people are receiving extra money based on sales, the company runs the risk of being driven by sales at the expense of profits." His point was that the company could underprice its product to generate lots of royalties for the two executives and in the process fail to generate profits for the investors.

He added: "The business plan would look better if you [the president and chief engineer] each had more stock. This royalty arrangement just makes you look greedy."

Investors also worry that special arrangements undermine team unity. Resentments inevitably accumulate if some executives are profiting from company sales or production and others aren't. Investors want to know that everyone is working toward the same goal—increasing sales and profits so as to increase the long-term value of the stock.

By the same token, investors take a dim view of executive salaries which exceed industry norms. High salaries, they reason, inevitably cut into profits and thus adversely affect the potential long-term value of the business.

As a general principle, especially in new companies, all employee compensation—including salaries, stock incentive plans, and profit-sharing programs—should be disclosed completely and concisely in the business plan.

3. *Use employment agreements.* Golden handcuffs can help keep and motivate key employees, but they are far from foolproof. Key employees may decide that they can just as easily use what they've learned at an existing company to command a higher salary at another company or to start their own busi-

ness. In starting another venture, they figure, they'll have 50% or more of their own business versus perhaps 5% to 20% of the company they are now with.

Investors look to employment agreements as added protection against key employees running off with all the product information, customer lists, and other goodies they have access to and either giving them to a competitor they've signed on with or using them to start a competing company. Employment agreements, then, should cover two broad areas: disclosure and competition.

Essentially, young businesses need to prevent their executives from disclosing such confidential information as product designs, production techniques, and plans for new products or services to competitors or to the general public via news articles. The businesses also need to prevent a key employee from going down the street to start the same kind of business. All executives, then, should be required, as a matter of course, to sign an employment agreement that limits disclosure and competition.

Company founders should be aware that they can provide limitations but not total prohibitions on key employees. Courts have ruled in recent years that key employees can't be arbitrarily prohibited from disclosing everything or competing at all and that such agreements can't go on forever. Employment agreements must be governed by some sense of reasonableness.

Thus, key executives might be prohibited from disclosing information about or using for competitive purposes such new product information as was stimulated by the company's needs; new products developed on the employee's own time which don't relate to the company's plans or business might be the right and property of the executive. A key employee of a coal-cleaning company, for instance, wrote into his employment agreement that products he developed with applications other than coal cleaning weren't covered by the non-disclosure and non-competition provisions.

Such agreements can be described in a sentence or two in the management-team section of the business plan and should be available to potential investors who will no doubt want to see the agreements as part of the "due diligence" effort.

Building on the Team

Entrepreneurs can add considerable value to their management team in investors' eyes by assembling a board of directors heavily weighted toward credible outsiders. Indeed, the notion of a blue-ribbon board is one of the most common suggestions panelists make at MIT Enterprise Forum sessions. This goes against the natural inclination of many entrepreneurs, who commonly make the board a rubber-stamp entity by limiting it to company insiders and perhaps the company's attorney and accountant.

Outside boards impress potential investors because such boards can legitimately help young growing companies grapple effectively with the many challenges of the early years. Moreover, outside boards are relatively inexpensive to assemble and maintain. Token payments of $50 or $100 a meeting (plus expenses) or group dinners or entertainment are usually enough to show appreciation for the service. Individuals inclined to serve usually understand the financial constraints on fledgling companies and, besides, tend to welcome the stimulation and challenge of being involved with young ventures. However, under these conditions, a board member will want equity in the company, usually 1% to 5%, to keep him or her interested in its problems and progress.

Who should comprise an effective and impressive outside

board? Retired executives, entrepreneurs who run noncompeting companies, business school professors, and key users of the company's product or service are among those who should be sought out. Criteria for selecting members should include both the individuals' past experience and current rapport with the venture's top executives.

Companies providing products or services which could incur liability suits—such as chemical or genetic engineering companies—might encounter resistance from potential board members, who fear being sued. In such cases, a board of advisers, independent of the board of directors, should be considered. The letter of invitation to board members should state that company executives have no obligation to accept members' opinions; the effect of saying that advisory board members have no legal power is to release the members from legal liability.

An effective board of directors or advisers enhances the management team and in so doing gives the young venture an additional advantage over competitors in the battle for capital. All board members should be listed in the business plan and half-page biographical sketches of each should be included in the appendix.

IN SUMMARY

The business plan's first section, which describes the company, must convey a sense that the fledgling company is being managed by experienced and savvy executives. Among the issues investors are most concerned about are the following:

- The business must be managed by a team—usually of three to six people—rather than by a single individual.
- The team members must have complementary rather than

similar managerial skills and must show evidence of appropriate previous business experience.

• Entrepreneurs must be both careful and creative in using stock and financial inducements to attract key team members.

• Teams can vary widely in their status, according to four levels, from most to least desirable:

Level 4, which has all team members identified and on board
Level 3, which has all members identified, but not necessarily on board
Level 2, which has one or two gaps in the team
Level 1, which has only one key manager

• Team members must be effectively motivated; among the most effective devices are golden handcuffs and employment agreements.

8

Those %&*#@!
Financial Projections

Investors routinely expect business plans to project sales, profits, and other financial results five years into the future. These projections are the keys to valuing the company, and thus they will determine how much of an enterprise investors expect in exchange for funding.

This isn't to say that investors, once they decide to back a company, simply accept its financial projections at face value. Entrepreneurs nearly always predict substantial sales and profit growth five years down the road. And in the actual experience of professional investors, fledgling companies nearly always fail to achieve their rosy projections.

According to Robert J. Crowley, a vice chairman of the MIT Enterprise Forum and vice president of Massachusetts Technology Development Corp. (MTDC), a major venture capital firm, none of the twenty-nine businesses his firm invested in through 1981 had met its financial projections in the three- to five-year period following investment. His analysis showed that the investees achieved between 20% and 80% of what had been projected; two investments failed completely.

Officials of four other major venture capital firms we surveyed unanimously agreed with Mr. Crowley. All said they were satisfied when investees reached 50% of their projected financial goals. They also agreed that the negotiations which determine the percentage of the company purchased by the investment dollars are affected by what might be called the "projection discount factor." As is the case with most transactions in this life, MTDC and the other venture capital firms have rarely been "long-changed."

If financial projections are so frequently off-target, entrepreneurs might ask, then why bother with them? Indeed, founders frequently ask that question at MIT Enterprise Forum sessions. After all, they wonder, how can anyone be expected to say what's going to happen three to five years into the future, particularly regarding something as volatile as a new or very young company.

One entrepreneur who was undergoing intense questioning by panelists about his company's projections finally said, in exasperation, "I really don't take our projections or any projections more than a year out all that seriously. After all, I don't really know how much business it's reasonable to expect three, four, and five years into the future."

A panelist's response was swift and certain. "We know you can't say for sure what's going to happen," the panelist observed. "But you must go through the thought process. You must consider best case and worst case scenarios. You must demonstrate that you can quantify the marketing, production, and other research and testing you've done. We may not agree with your projections, but we want to see that you've thought about where your company might be in five years and quantified your thinking."

Indeed, a company's financial projections are the *result* of its strategy and planning. After the founders have determined what they and their company want to be when they grow up, after they have done extensive marketing research, and after they have figured out what resources, people, production, and capital must be assembled—then and only then can the financial projections be calculated and put into written form. The company's future is quantified in its projections (as modified by the "projection discount factor").

If investors are impressed with the business plan's presentation of the venture concept, they will consider the financial projections critically and with great care. Both the investors themselves and the financial consultants they hire will examine every line item. Incorrect entries, exaggerated items, and missing categories will be picked up in the "due diligence" process and could be used to rule out an investment. At a minimum, investors will identify both conceptual and actual errors and raise questions which could damage—or even abort—investment negotiations.

This chapter evaluates where business plans commonly go wrong in assembling financial projections and describes the contents of complete financial plans. Together with evaluation criteria described in the previous two chapters, this chapter leads to the Rich-Gumpert Evaluation System immediately following to explain how investors decide what percentage of companies will be purchased at what price.

Unwise Manipulation

Once they realize there's no way around making financial projections, entrepreneurs tend to go to extremes in the numbers they offer. In some cases, they don't do enough, relying on figures that are skimpy and, most often, so overly optimistic that anyone who has read more than a dozen business plans quickly sees through such numbers.

In one MIT Enterprise Forum presentation, a management

team proposing to manufacture and market scientific instruments came up with a net profit after taxes of 25% of sales revenues In the fourth and fifth years following investment. Although a few industries, such as computer software, have experienced such extreme profits, the business of producing scientific instruments is so competitive, panelists noted, that such margins are unrealistically high.

One panelist who examined the financials in detail found that important costs were grossly—and carelessly—understated. Panelists advised the company officials to take their financial estimates back to the drawing board before approaching investors, so that the business plan wouldn't be rejected out of hand.

At another extreme are entrepreneurs who think that the financials *are* the business plan. Such entrepreneurs tend to cover the business plan with a smog of numbers. These "spreadsheet merchants," with pages and pages of computer printout covering every variation possible in business and product sensitivity analyses, completely turn off many investors.

A partner in a major Massachusetts venture capital firm has told us that he welcomes a set of solid financial projections going to five years after the investment, with perhaps one set of variations to illustrate that the business won't go down the tubes if conditions are not quite as optimistic as calculated in the basic plan. He notes that inclusion of one or two dozen financial spreadsheets in the business plan immediately makes him negative about the entire plan. Generally speaking, "spreadsheetitis" is a new computer-age disease that needs a cold-turkey cure.

As investors are aware, financial projections are usually overly optimistic, but they are certainly no place for false modesty. To illustrate this point, it's useful to consider a presentation made to the MIT Enterprise Forum, in which the management team of a computer software company projected a sales and profit growth rate of 25% annually, believing it was presenting itself as "attractively conservative." This led to an annual sales level of only about $5 million, with profits of $500,000 after five years—figures far too low to attract venture capital investment, especially in the computer software field.

Computer software companies have been among the hottest growth groups in the United States during the early and middle 1980s, and they continue to have explosive growth potential. As one extreme example, Lotus Development, producers of Lotus 1-2-3, went from nothing to $60 million annual sales in two years. Thus, growth to $5 million annually in five years seemed quite pale by comparison. Being conservative for the sake of appearances is somewhat like false humility—detectable and not very attractive.

(Most venture capital groups are seeking a minimum of $20 million of sales revenues within five years from their investments.)

Aside from the negative reactions unrealistic projections create, entrepreneurs must keep in mind that their estimates of profitability in five years are extremely important in laying the groundwork for negotiating the percentage of the company that the investors will receive in return for their money. Moreover, financial forecasts are viewed by investors essentially as promises by founders that are a yardstick by which to judge performance.

Some investment deals are structured to reward the management team which meets or exceeds its forecasts—and penalize the team if it fails to match its projections (such as by giving investors authority to replace officers or to buy additional stock at discount prices). Bonuses, royalties, stock options, or warrants can be tied to performance versus projections. Clearly, management's best interests are served by preparing pro forma financials which are realizable—and still attractive enough to win investment.

What to Include

Most investors expect financial projections to extend five years from the date of the investment—five years being a type of magic number within which almost all businesses are expected to be profitable. Customarily, all the projections except the balance sheet show a monthly progression over the first two years and a quarterly progression for the remaining three years. The balance sheets can be provided on a quarterly basis during the first two years and on a semi-annual basis thereafter. (See sample charts on pages 158–160.)

The specific financial projections that are expected in a business plan and the items they consist of are as follows:

1. *The Income Statement* (Profit and Loss) should include the following basic elements:

Sales
Cost of Sales
  Material
  Labor
  Overhead
  Total
Gross Margin (Sales less Cost of Sales)
Operating Expenses:
  Marketing, Selling Costs
  Research and Development
  General and Administrative
  Total
Income (Loss) from Operations

Interest Income (Expense)
Income (Loss) before Taxes
Taxes on Income
Net Income (Loss)

Some operational footnotes should be included on the income statement to explain how certain totals were arrived at. Also, gross margins should be calculated as a percentage of sales; any significant deviation from industry norms must be explained.

2. *The Cash Flow Forecast* should include the following basic elements:

Beginning Cash Balance
Cash Receipts
    Collection of Receivables
    Interest Income
    Total
Cash Disbursements:
    Accounts Payable
    Payments of Other Expenses
    Income Tax Payments
    Total
Net Cash from (Used for) Operations
Sale of Stock
Purchase of Equipment
Decrease (Increase) in Funds Invested
Short-term Borrowings (Repayments)
Ending Cash Balance

The Cash Flow Forecast is extremely useful to management in *anticipating* problems—or successes. It should be updated monthly to help guide the managers in their decision making.

3. *The Balance Sheet* should include the following basic elements:

Assets:
  Current Assets
    Cash
    Investments
    Accounts Receivable
    Inventory
    Total
  Property, Plant and Equipment
  Total Assets
Liabilities and Stockholders' Equity:
  Current Liabilities
    Short-term Debt
    Accounts Payable
    Income Taxes Payable
    Accrued Liabilities
    Total
  Long-term Debt
  Stockholders' Equity
    Preferred Stock
    Common Stock
    Retained Earnings (Deficit)
    Total
  Total Liabilities and Stockholders' Equity

The pro forma balance sheets help investors evaluate entrepreneurs' appreciation of corporate asset management. The approach should conform with conventional accounting practice so that the sheets are readable and credible.

4. *Break-Even Analysis.* This consists of a chart, usually linear, showing total costs versus total sales, over a period of time, usually months and years. Break-even is achieved when total sales equal total costs. The time at which this is

achieved is of vital interest to both investors and management, since it helps both groups assess financing needs.

Making the Numbers Believable

Investors compare the financial projections that become a part of any seriously considered business plan with others in the same industry. Investors will make the comparison—if they aren't already familiar with the industry—by quickly obtaining annual reports and 10K and other documents that all public companies must file yearly with the Securities and Exchange Commission (SEC). If some aspect of the projections is far out of line with others in the same industry, investors will want to know why.

An entrepreneur at an MIT Enterprise Forum session showed R&D expenditures for his specialty chemical venture equaling about half of gross sales revenues. A panelist had gone to the trouble of obtaining annual reports and 10K's from comparable organic chemical suppliers. Why, he asked the presenter, were the company's R&D expenditures so much higher than others in the industry, which typically spent about 5% of gross revenues for research and development?

The presenter mentioned how he wanted the company to continually develop new products in its field, which necessitated the high R&D expenditure. Although his purpose was admirable, the panel unanimously advised the entrepreneur to bring the company's R&D expenditures into line with the rest of the industry. The presenter ignored the advice—and the company failed to obtain needed financing and eventually discontinued operations.

The same principle holds true for sales expenses, general and administrative overhead, legal and patent counsel expenditures, accounting and auditing, and so forth. Evaluating the debt-equity ratio in a new business by comparison with those established in the industry is more difficult. However, a company which has been in its industry for several years and is seeking to expand its operations will find obtaining additional investment to be helped if the company does not deviate too significantly from industry norms, even in its debt-equity ratio.

Investors will also examine compensation of company officers as it affects motivation and loyalty versus draining of company resources. A clear conflict exists between these two extremes. The investors want to see that the company executives are properly motivated so that they won't leave the company for some other opportunity. Yet the investors also want to see their money go into marketing, sales, and manufacturing rather than salaries so as to provide cash flow and profit as soon as possible.

To counter these concerns, you should examine the annual reports and other records of companies in the same field and seek to provide the officers with salaries smaller—to some degree—than those provided by larger, established companies. The developing company can make up the difference with options that will more than compensate for the sacrifice when the management team brings the company to the level of success that is projected in the business plan. For example, if the vice president for engineering of an established company in the same field as the emerging enterprise receives a salary of, say, $75,000 a year, the emerging company wouldn't be out of line to provide its vice president for engineering with $55,000 a year plus options that would be vested over a five-year period so that, if all goes as predicted, the officer would realize a net capital gain of perhaps half a million dollars.

Bonus incentives based upon profits can also increase salaries and not reduce the value of the options. Such incentives, over a modest salary base, in place of high guaranteed salaries reduce the general and administrative overhead drain during the venture's projected major growth period.

A way of detailing and justifying staffing decisions and expenses in the business plan is via a single-page staffing chart, showing the types of personnel required by the company over time. Such a chart indicates the planning capabilities of the management team besides furnishing support for the wages and salaries accounted for in the income statement and cash-flow projections. Backup information should be available separately or in the second volume of supporting detail.

Finally, you must face up to the issue of formulating the sales projections. They are based on the market research and testing activities presented in summarized detail in earlier sections of the business plan. As we noted in Chapter 4 on marketing, no sophisticated investor will be impressed with such statements as, "In this huge market, we'll easily get at least 5%, which is $50 million annually in a $1 billion market."

The monthly, quarterly, and annual sales revenues must be shown to be based upon customer reactions to the user benefits. Factors such as the specific market niche and the maximum number of customer prospects, identified in a credible manner, must be figured into sales calculations, with reasonable supporting data which can be examined critically at a later time during the "due diligence" period.

You can use many types of data on which to base reasonable sales projections. You can interview a sample of prospective customers, issue a product release to appropriate trade publications to gauge response, and exhibit at trade shows to obtain reaction to products. We cannot emphasize too strongly that prospective investors will examine critically the credibility of the sales figures in the projected profit-and-loss statement.

Putting the Tables Together

Pages 158–160 show some typical formats of projections to illustrate the degree of completeness investors consider customary. These statements represent the sorts of detail investors view as expected in projections. Naturally, businesses vary, so certain of the details will vary from one business plan to another.

These pro forma financial tables are conventional and, in being so, make an important point: All financials presented to investors must be as "investor friendly" as possible. That is, the financial projections should be in a form that is customarily presented in annual reports, business plans, and 10K statements.

Although the fledgling company's products or services may well be innovative, the financial projections never should be. More important, the financial projections should reinforce investor confidence concerning management's financial competence. Thus, they should be carefully reviewed, first by the company accountant and then by a friendly venture capitalist and banker—all of whom should be invited to criticize the presentation and compare it with ideal models.

The financial projections must speak for themselves. They should not require interpretation and should not raise questions extraneous to the business itself. Explanations should be limited to the customary simple footnotes to financials. The sample tables follow.

Company Name
Pro Forma Monthly Income Statement
198_ ($ 000)

Month
Item
Sales Revenues
  Sales Allowances
Net Revenues
Cost of Goods Sold
  Material
  Labor
  Overhead
Total
Gross Margin

Operating Expenses
  Selling
    Salaries
    Advertising
    Other
  General-Administrative
  Research and Development
  Depreciation
Total
Income (Loss) from Operations
Interest Income (Expense)
Net Income (Loss)
Provision for Taxes
Net Income after Taxes
Net Increase (Decrease) to Retained Earnings

Company Name
Pro Forma Monthly Cash Flow Statement
198_ ($ 000)

Month
Item
Beginning Cash Balance
Receipts
   Collection of Receivables
   Interest Income
   Other
Total Receipts

Cash Disbursements
   Accounts Payable
   Direct Materials
   Direct Labor
   Equipment
   Salaries
   Rent
   Insurance
   Advertising
   Taxes
   Loan Payments
   Other

Total Disbursements
Total Cash Flow
Ending Cash Balance

Company Name
Pro Forma Balance Sheet
Year Ending 198_ ($ 000)

Quarter
Item
ASSETS
Current Assets
  Cash
  Accounts Receivable (less
  allowance for doubtful accounts)
  Net Accounts Receivable
  Notes Receivable
  Inventory
  Prepaid Expenses
  Other
  Total Current Assets
Fixed Assets
  Land
  Buildings
  Equipment
  Total Net Fixed Assets
  Other Assets
TOTAL ASSETS

LIABILITIES
Current Liabilities
  Accounts Payable
  Notes Payable
  Taxes Payable
  Other
  Total Current Liabilities
Long-term Liabilities
  Equity
  Withdrawals
Net Equity
TOTAL LIABILITY AND EQUITY

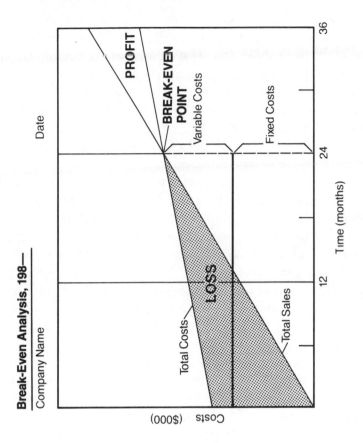

How Much of the Company Must We Give Up?

This question is frequently uppermost in the minds of entrepreneurs. It came up at a recent MIT Enterprise Forum session when an entrepreneur seeking funds for an office automation company said he wanted advice from panelists on "How our company can raise a substantial amount of money without the founders losing control."

Panelists sought to reassure the entrepreneur, arguing that, from the investor's perspective, the issue is meaningless. "If you're doing a good job, you're in control," observed one panelist. "If you're not doing a good job, the bankers or venture capitalists are in control."

A second panelist noted, "The venture capitalist is looking to maximize investment gains, not for control."

A third panelist, an official of a large venture capital firm, seconded those observations, pointing out that excessive focus by entrepreneurs on the control issue can turn investors off. "We were about ready to invest in a startup company," she recalled. "We sat down with the founders, and the president talked for half an hour about how he and the others wanted to keep 51% of the company before it went public. He said he didn't care about control after the company went public. But we decided he was too interested in control. We're interested in growing a substantial company. Control isn't the issue. So we decided against backing that company."

Indeed, dilution is an inevitable by-product of outside investment. Because entrepreneurs worry so much about their ownership being reduced, they often either avoid seeking outside investment or do not make a truly strong effort to obtain the funding they may legitimately need.

But founders must keep in mind that the last thing investors want is to provide new management for an emerging enterprise. Investors, regardless of the percentage of a company they own, will avoid replacing the people who created a business unless they prove totally incompetent. In that case, replacement is best for all concerned, including the founders.

IN SUMMARY

The businooo plan must project financial data five years into the future. Although investors expect that the projections will turn out in practice to have been optimistic, the investors also expect the data to be logical, well researched, and carefully assembled. Financial projections should include the following:

• The income statement, showing sales, gross margin, expenses, and income or loss

• The cash-flow forecast, showing receipts and disbursements over time, and the expected real time requirements for cash

• The balance sheet, showing assets and liabilities

• The break-even analysis, showing when total sales and costs become equal, after which the business will generate profits

The financial data must also conform in presentation and in the scope of sales and expenses with those of other companies in the same industry and with generally accepted accounting formats.

The Rich-Gumpert
Evaluation System

Having studied the methods for creating the business plan, how can you anticipate the strengths and weaknesses of the plan yourself—before it reaches your audience. Here is our system for rating investment opportunities: your own or any venture.

The various ideas behind our approach aren't necessarily new or original to investors, who have long applied at least some of them in their own efforts to pick winners. But, to our knowledge, no investors, consultants, or other business experts have put the various disparate ideas together into a single overall system for evaluating fledgling enterprises. Indeed, we have described the system to a number of investment experts whose judgment we respect and all have enthusiastically embraced it as innovative and useful.

Although we are, of course, somewhat biased, we feel the system we have devised is useful to all who are concerned with understanding young companies. Entrepreneurs can use the system to give them an indication of where they stand in investors' minds. Investors can use the system to add a new dimension to the qualitative and quantitative analysis they do in assessing businesses.

Our evaluation system is essentially a two-step process, as follows:

1. First comes a qualitative assessment, based on the status of the product and the management team, as described in Chapters 6 and 7. Thus, most desirable is what we might refer to as a "4/4"—a business with a Level 4 product and a Level 4 management team. This venture has an accepted product in a proven market, run by a first-class and fully staffed management team and is clearly the likeliest combination to win investment funds at the lowest cost for the money.

At the other extreme is a single entrepreneur with an unproven idea—a 1/1. This venture has barely a chance to obtain investment funds unless the founder has a magnificent track record. All of the other combinations will range between these extremes (as illustrated in the table on page 169).

Entrepreneurs who become aware of their rating and feel it inadequate can then work to improve it. Take the case of two entrepreneurs who approached an Enterprise Forum executive committee member with a plan for a business which would produce recorded cassette tapes of information for senior executives. The two entrepreneurs simply had an idea for the tapes' format and content, but they had never produced a tape. That put them at Level 1 in terms of product development.

The entrepreneurs each had previous marketing and financial experience, but neither had experience developing the product they were proposing. Thus, they were missing a product manager—in this case an editor to select and assemble material for the tapes. That put them at Level 2 in terms of their management team.

This particular business plan was, in our system, a 1/2. When told by the executive committee member that the business was probably not far enough along to attract investment capital, the entrepreneurs went about seeking to correct the situation. First, they obtained a commitment from an experienced editor to help develop a prototype tape and join the company as an employee after investment funds were obtained. Then the three individuals went about producing a prototype that could be manufactured in quantity.

Those actions moved the company up to Level 3 in terms of both product development and management team, making it a 3/3 instead of a 1/2. The team revised its business plan to take into account these important changes and quickly attracted interest from potential investors.

Many venture capitalists will invest only in 4/4 companies because, clearly, the risk is minimized with a proven product and a complete management team. However, a growing number of venture capital firms are actively seeking out 3/3 and even 2/2 situations. (Trends among venture capitalists and other investors are described in detail in Chapter 9.)

We must emphasize, though, that these ratings must take into account the quality of the achievement levels. Thus, a 4/4 enterprise producing a product or service that has customers who have some significant complaints about it or one managed by an inexperienced team might have its rating downgraded—such as to 4-C/4-C. Or, if the product or service is excellent and clearly has an exciting future, it can be graded "A," and so on.

Similarly, a 2/2 enterprise with a model of an exciting new computer graphics system being started by two entrepreneurs who had successfully started and sold out of a similar company (profitably) a few years before might have a real-life rating of 2-A/2-A. This latter enterprise might have a better chance of obtaining funding than the previous enterprise.

Although such an additional dimension is too cumbersome to include in the table of our basic system, entrepreneurs must also assess and, if possible, raise their qualitative rating within the evaluation system.

2. Once Investors know where a company stands qualitatively, they can begin to do some quantitative analysis. As we have noted, investors seek an annual return on investment in the range of 35% to more than 60%, compounded, net of inflation. Because risk and return are closely related, 4/4 companies can rightfully be expected to yield in the 35% to 40% range, while 2/2 companies are often expected to yield 60%.

As we have mentioned, one of the customary ways to calculate the value of an enterprise is on the basis of the expected results in the fifth year following investment. For a 4/4 company expected to yield 35% annually, investors would be seeking 4.5 times their original investment, before inflation, over a five-year period.

Investors thus need to calculate the potential worth of the company after five years and determine what percentage of the company they must own to realize their return. Carrying our 4/4 example further, the investors may decide after allowing for the "projection discount factor" that the company will have $20 million annual revenues after five years and a net profit of $1.5 million. Based on a conventional multiple for acquisitions of 10 times earnings, it would be worth $15 million in five years.

Assuming that the company is seeking $1 million of financing, that amount should be worth $4.5 million after five years to satisfy investors. To realize $4.5 million from a company worth $15 million, the investors would need to own a bit less than one-third of the company. However, if inflation during the five-year period is expected to average 7.5% a year, investors would be looking for a value of $6.46 million as a reasonable return over five years, or 43% of the company.

Thus, the final percentage of the company acquired by the

investors is subject to some negotiation, depending on the projected earnings of the company and the expected rate of inflation.

For a 2/2 investment, from which investors would be seeking 60% annually, net of inflation, a $1 million investment would have to bring close to $15 million in five years, with inflation figured at 7.5% annually. Few businesses can make a convincing case for such a rich return on investment if they don't already have a product that is in the hands of some representative customers.

Although the approach we have just described is typical, it is not necessarily universal. Some investors are less rigid in their venture valuation process. One venture capitalist told an MIT Enterprise Forum workshop on buying and selling companies that, although he goes through the procedure we have just described, he believes that valuation is mainly subjective. He gets a feeling about the entrepreneurs from their business plan, the "due diligence" process, and repeated contacts. He then decides whether he wants to bet on them strongly, with average intensity, or not at all. During negotiations with companies, he considers how badly the business needs the money versus how badly he and his fellow investors want to buy in. The price is arrived at accordingly.

Some investors only back businesses which show promise of becoming profitable in a very short time, such as two to three years. Computer software firms have demonstrated the ability to meet such expectations. Investors in such situations will typically seek a higher annual rate of return than otherwise to justify the time and effort associated with evaluating the venture; but the overall return expected will still be less than would be "normal" after five years, thus reducing the percentage of the company investors will seek to acquire.

In the other direction are very large capital equipment–type

The Rich-Gumpert Evaluation System

Note: The *quality* of the product/service and the management team will increase or decrease the desirability of the investment.

MOST DESIRABLE ⟶

PRODUCT/SERVICE STATUS					MOST DESIRABLE
LEVEL 4 Product/service fully developed. Many satisfied users. Market established.	$4/1$	$4/2$	$4/3$	$4/4$	
LEVEL 3 Product/service fully developed. Few (or no) users as yet. Market assumed.	$3/1$	$3/2$	$3/3$	$3/4$	
LEVEL 2 Product/service pilot operable. Not yet developed for production. Market assumed.	$2/1$	$2/2$	$2/3$	$2/4$	
LEVEL 1 A product or service idea, but not yet operable. Market assumed.	$1/1$	$1/2$	$1/3$	$1/4$	
	LEVEL 1 A single, would-be founder-entrepreneur.	**LEVEL 2** Two founders. Additional slots, personnel not identified.	**LEVEL 3** Partly staffed management team. Absent members identified, to join when firm is funded.	**LEVEL 4** Fully staffed, experienced management team.	

MANAGEMENT STATUS

investments which require five to ten years before they can be expected to become seriously profitable. Investors will become involved in these only when they feel confident the company has the potential to become a giant, with the resulting major returns to founders and investors.

It's safe to conclude, then, that the process of valuing a young business is at once a logical and an arbitrary process. It is logical in that it takes into account informed estimates of financial results and the company's progress in developing its product and assembling a management team. It is arbitrary in the sense that no one can know for sure how events in a young company will unfold.

It's certainly clear that if the company does better than expected financially, both founders and investors benefit. If the company does worse than expected, both groups lose. Or, as investors like to say, it's much nicer to own 10% of a $100 million company than 50% of a $5 million company. Entrepreneurs who keep sight of that fundamental truth are ready to proceed to the process of shopping for money—the subject of our next chapter.

9

Shopping for Funds

Entrepreneurs can spend many months writing and rewriting the business plan to put it into topnotch form, but they can waste that effort if the plan doesn't make its way into the hands of the most appropriate financiers.

Finding the right backers is a task that often becomes quite complex, because financiers come in all sizes, shapes, and flavors—so many as to be nearly overwhelming. A few statistics help tell the story. There are about 14,000 commercial banks, more than 600 private venture capital firms, and untold thousands of private investors. They all vary according to the size and type of company they'll back as well as to the amount of financing they'll extend. There's no way any venture can check out all the options.

Entrepreneurs, then, must resolve three basic issues. First, they must decide whether to seek investment or debt funds. Second, entrepreneurs must target their efforts to the investor or lender firms likeliest to back their type of venture. And third, they must find ways to effectively reach the targeted financiers.

This chapter examines the decision of which type of financing to seek, explores the different kinds of financiers, and offers advice on making contacts with financial backers. Failure to resolve these issues can doom even the most promising enterprise.

Little Room for Error

The business-plan preparation process usually takes longer than entrepreneurs expect—from two to six months is typical, with the actual amount of time dependent on the team's expertise and the tasks required to make the business attractive to financiers. Thus, fledgling companies are in many cases quite short of cash when the plan is finally ready to show to potential backers.

It's not uncommon for the evaluation and negotiation process, even when it goes smoothly, to consume another three to six months. Barking up too many of the wrong financial trees thus wastes precious time and energy at a time when the venture can least afford it.

As the head of one startup venture which had spent several months unsuccessfully shopping its business plan around to venture capitalists stated at an MIT Enterprise Forum session, "We're getting to the end of our fuse. We've done all the begging, borrowing, and stealing we can. Not only does the company desperately need money, but we (the management team) need to eat."

At first glance, the easier of the shopping issues to resolve is the first—whether to seek investment or debt funds. But existing companies, in particular, sometimes find that issue difficult to resolve. Too often, they want to avoid burdening their companies with debt and they also want to be part of what they perceive to be the more glamorous venture capital process.

The president of a year-old company producing and selling a patented device which enables conveyor belts to operate more efficiently than otherwise appeared at an MIT Enterprise Forum session in such a circumstance. He couldn't understand that investors were unwilling to put up $1 million of funds his company needed to fill existing orders and expand capacity for new ones.

Panelists noted that while they were extremely impressed with the company's management team and felt the business plan to be a credible document, the company didn't make a convincing enough case that it would yield the 35% to 60% annual returns investors seek over three to seven years. One panelist gave this advice: "Since you have orders on the books, though, you might try to stretch your banking relationships. For instance, you might try to do receivables financing [whereby a bank loans funds against the amount due from the orders that have been filled and shipped to customers]."

Because lenders are primarily concerned about the existence of collateral, companies which have equipment, property, inventory, orders, or other such tangibles should first consider obtaining loans. For startup companies, collateral is more difficult to come by; it can come in the form of the equity in one's house, life insurance cash value, and stocks, but many entrepreneurs are understandably reluctant to risk their entire financial worth for a business loan.

Companies which expect to grow at a rate greater than 35% annually and companies without enough collateral to cover loans as a source of the financing they seek should turn to investors. Because investors are concerned primarily with ventures' future growth prospects, their interest tends to be focused on businesses in emerging areas or industries—electronics, robotics, telecommunications, genetic engineering, computers, and franchising, among other possibilities. In addition, fast-growth companies, even if they have some collateral, are often best off avoiding heavy dependence on loans to avoid straining their usually tight cash-flow situations.

It's also possible for young businesses to obtain some combination of debt and equity funding. Such funding comes most commonly from small business investment companies (SBIC's)—a type of venture capital firm which itself borrows funds from the Small Business Administration and thus tries to generate both immediate income from interest on loans and long-term profits from investments. And as lending competition heats up, increasing numbers of commercial lenders are experimenting with debt-equity packages.

Once entrepreneurs settle on either investment or debt financing, how do they go about selecting financier candidates? That is, how do they sort out the various choices to obtain funds at satisfactory terms in the shortest time possible?

First, it's important to keep in mind that both investors and lenders have certain preferences about the companies they want to back. These preferences are usually based on the type, history, and status of the company and the amount of financing needed.

Also worth noting is that both investors and lenders are increasingly willing to get involved with young small ventures. That isn't to say that officials of such businesses will be wined and dined, or even treated respectfully, wherever they go in search of funds. But investors will generally consider early-stage ventures more seriously than they were inclined to a few years ago. And many large banks have established special departments to deal with small company borrowers.

We'll first evaluate investor choices and then consider lender options.

Targeting Investors

Investors can be divided into four broad categories, as follows:

1. *Traditional venture capitalists.* Increasing numbers of emerging growth companies are receiving funding from the rapidly expanding venture capital industry. By the mid-1980s, the nation's more than six hundred venture capital firms had several billion dollars available for investment, compared with only about $50 million available in 1977. Venture capital firms have benefited in large measure from reductions in the capital gains tax rate, which has encouraged insurance companies, pension funds, and wealthy families like the Rockefellers, Paysons, and Whitneys to make funds available for investment.

Though the venture capital industry is a young one, it has become increasingly sophisticated since the 1950s, when American Research and Development Corporation, the first venture capital firm, invested $70,000 in a new company known as Digital Equipment Corporation; that investment eventually mushroomed into the hundreds of millions of dollars and still stands as one of the most successful ever made anywhere.

Today's venture capitalists rely nearly exclusively on written business plans to evaluate investments. They resist interviews before reading business plans for a couple of reasons. First, they don't want to be influenced by their initial reactions to entrepreneurs' personalities. Second, venture capitalists just don't have the time to spend forty-five minutes or an hour listening to an entrepreneur describe his or her business when they can spend a few minutes reading the executive summary and other key points of a business plan and probably learn more.

Traditional venture capitalists will typically invest anywhere from $250,000 to $1.5 million in an enterprise. If a business appears particularly promising, but requires perhaps $4 million or $5 million of financing, then three to five firms will often join forces to put up the funds. They invariably prefer enterprises at the Level 4 stage in both product development and management team, though they are increasingly receptive to businesses at the Level 3 stage in one or the other area (4/3's or 3/4's).

Venture capital firms actually come in three forms: private firms, which get their support from insurance companies, pension funds, and wealthy families; small business investment companies (SBIC's), which are funded by a combination of Small Business Administration loans and private funds; and corporate venture capital firms, which are funded by individual Fortune 500 corporations.

Private venture capital firms are engaged in funding some of the most glamorous emerging industries, such as genetic engineering, robotics, and computer software. SBIC's typically fund more mature 4/4 situations, often with a combination of debt and equity. And corporate venture capital firms have become a steadily less influential factor in the marketplace as corporations have encountered difficulties negotiating with entrepreneurs and deciding on how such investments fit in with corporate goals; many corporations have thus reduced or eliminated their investments.

2. *Early-stage venture capital funds.* Up until the early 1980s, private venture capital firms would talk much about their willingness to back startup and early-stage enterprises—those at the Level 3 stage of product development and management team—but would put their money almost entirely into 4/4 companies. Their reasoning was simple: They wanted entrepreneurs to keep sending along business plans for startup situations on the off chance that one or two might prove irre-

sistible, but mostly they laid off because of fears over the risks involved.

But when Edward Roberts, an MIT professor (and a member of the MIT Enterprise Forum executive committee) who has done extensive research on entrepreneurship, conducted a study which found that more than 80% of high-technology companies in the Boston area survive at least five years, concerns over the risk of investing in such fledgling businesses diminished. During the early and mid-1980s, more than a dozen venture capital funds sprang up to specialize in investing in startup and very early stage companies.

These early stage funds usually limit their investments to between $50,000 and $250,000. By getting in so early, the venture capitalists expect to obtain a relatively substantial chunk of the young company—sometimes up to 50%—at a relatively low cost.

Such funds will usually limit their investments to companies at Level 3 or 4 in terms of product development and management team. That is, the products are ready or nearly ready for manufacture and sale and a management team is complete or nearly complete.

3. *Investment bankers.* These are the firms—some of which are huge Wall Street institutions like Paine, Webber and Merrill Lynch, and others of which are small local firms—that specialize in packaging young companies to go public and thereby raise the capital they need.

Traditionally, fledgling companies haven't gone public until they've achieved a track record of impressive sales growth and profitability. But in recent years, the notion of enterprises going public at a very early stage of development—before they've achieved significant sales and profitability—has become more acceptable. Of course, the possibilities for fund-raising success depend in large part on the stock market climate; a bull market is a prerequisite for emerging companies.

The process isn't an easy one. Entrepreneurs, together with investment bankers, must assemble a prospectus which conforms with strict Securities and Exchange Commission regulations regarding disclosure. The business plan can be extremely useful in writing the prospectus, but because the prospectus is a legal document, it must be extremely precise and cautious in what is promised; that is, investors must be warned explicitly about the various risks associated with backing a young inexperienced business. The whole procedure can take many months, by which time the stock market climate may have changed adversely.

But investment experts sometimes advise companies having difficulty obtaining venture capital funds to consider raising funds from the public via the investment banking route. As one panelist told an entrepreneur who was complaining at an MIT Enterprise Forum session about the problems of raising venture capital: "We are in an insane stock market at this time, and investment bankers are literally drooling over the possibilities of selling stock in companies like yours. The public is not as sophisticated as venture capitalists, so you can potentially raise a good deal of money from this source."

4. *Informal investors.* These are the individual investors who provide the seed, or startup capital, that gets many new enterprises off the ground. The term "informal investors" was coined by William Wetzel, a University of New Hampshire business school professor, who made a pioneering study of individual investors in New England in the early 1980s.

Not surprisingly, he found that informal investors are a difficult group to research. After all, there's no listing or association of informal investors; they are mostly wealthy individuals or groups of such people looking for new investment opportunities.

Possibly because of their wealth, they tend to value their privacy. Thus, Mr. Wetzel had to work very hard for his findings. He sent out more than 10,000 brochures describing his research to potential informal investors and followed up with questionnaires. He eventually wound up with 133 responses from investors.

Two researchers in California, Elna R. Tymes and O. J. Krasner of Pepperdine University, followed up Mr. Wetzel's research with a survey of their own on the West Coast and wound up with forty-one completed questionnaires. Their results were fairly similar to those obtained by Mr. Wetzel.

The two studies concluded that informal investors generally put up anywhere from $10,000 to $100,000 per investment, though there's an emphasis on the $10,000 to $25,000 range. The investors like to reduce their risk by investing together with other informal investors, so that the total amount available via this avenue can easily exceed $100,000.

The investors like startup and early-stage situations most—Level 3 and even Level 2 in product development and management team—preferably in manufacturing and high-technology fields, the studies found. And the backers expect to be able to liquidate their investments in five to seven years.

They also like to keep their investments within fifty miles of their homes and seek annual returns of between 20% and 50%. Interestingly, the Wetzel study found that investors might make an allowance in their returns to go under the 35% we have referred to as the minimum acceptable if the venture offers the hope of significantly helping the local community, such as by generating impressive numbers of jobs.

Informal investors sometimes use a couple of tax-reducing

devices through which to make their investments. The most popular of these are Research and Development Limited Partnerships and Subchapter S Corporations. R&D Limited Partnerships enable investors to realize tax advantages from operating losses during the initial product development period and then to obtain income based on royalties from patents or other research developments stemming from use of the original funds.

Subchapter S Corporations enable investors to write off on their personal taxes losses in the developing business's early years in proportion to their ownership of stock. Once the business makes money, the profits flow also in proportion to ownership, and they are then taxable. Entrepreneurs who locate potential informal investors and want to use one of these devices to entice potential backers into making the final commitment should consult with an accountant and attorney as to which device might be most appropriate and how to use it properly.

Within each of these four groups, investors can be further broken down according to the types of companies each prefers. As investors achieve success with companies in a particular industry or area, they pick up important information and knowledge about the success criteria of such companies. That explains why some investors limit themselves to investing exclusively in computer software companies while others specialize in telecommunications businesses.   ·

Some investors will consider a variety of possible ventures within certain marketing categories. For instance, a few venture capital firms have sprung up in recent years to concentrate their efforts on consumer product companies, an area venture capitalists had in the past avoided.

Other informal investors and venture capitalists continue to be generalists in approach, believing that they can spot winning and losing qualities in enterprises from a variety of industries. But even these investors tend to have a preference for certain areas, such as high-technology, and a distaste for certain areas, such as retailing or construction.

The book, *Guide to Venture Capital Sources,* by Stanley Pratt (Venture Economics, Wellesley Hills, MA), lists nearly all the traditional and early-stage venture capital firms and many investment bankers specializing in small company underwritings, along with the kinds of businesses the firms prefer to back. It is thus useful in providing names of potential sources to possibly approach, according to guidelines described later in this chapter. Unfortunately, no book or other single source keeps tabs on informal investors.

Targeting Lenders

Lenders don't break down as neatly as investors insofar as the kinds of companies they'll back are concerned. Although they do have fairly narrow financial guidelines for granting loans, individual banks and government agencies may make loans to businesses of a wide range of sizes and in a wide range of industries.

Broadly speaking, we can divide lenders into two categories:

1. *Commercial lenders.* This category includes commercial banks, commercial finance companies, factors, leasing companies, and insurance companies. Thanks to deregulation of commercial banking and the impressive growth exhibited by many small companies, commercial lenders have become increasingly interested in making loans to smaller companies. Indeed, many commercial banks offer special seminar and

consulting services to smaller companies in efforts to attract their loan business.

Because commercial lenders are primarily interested in seeing their loans repaid, they examine most closely the assets and cash flow of potential lenders. They differ in the sorts of collateral they prefer. For instance, bankers prefer machinery and real estate, while commercial lenders like accounts receivable and inventory. Leasing companies don't look for collateral as much as they do evidence of continuing and strong cash flow, to enable companies to keep up on their lease payments.

For all practical purposes, commercial lenders will only deal with companies at Level 4 both in their product development and management team. And in many cases, they'll insist that the company have been in business a minimum amount of time—say two or three years.

Loans are usually limited to the amount of collateral that can be offered. And loans must usually be repaid within five years, though increasing numbers of banks are allowing loans to stretch as long as ten years.

Although commercial lenders are interested in all the areas described in previous chapters as being important for the business plan, they want greater detail in certain areas than investors would usually require. This detail includes valuations of machinery, real estate, and inventory along with lists of customers and the owners' personal assets.

Commercial lenders commonly have their own loan applications. Entrepreneurs who can provide lenders with a business plan based on the principles of this book along with a completed loan application can go a long way toward enhancing their chances for obtaining funds. Because as closely as lenders look at collateral and cash flow, they also want to be reassured that the borrowers are savvy managers.

2. *Government lenders.* The most famous government lender is the Small Business Administration. Ironically, during recent years the SBA has nearly removed itself from making direct loans of government funds to small businesses. Instead, it relies on commercial banks to make loans on its behalf; the agency then guarantees repayment of up to 90% of the amount should borrowers default.

The agency has in recent years guaranteed up to $3 billion annually of bank loans. And increasingly, the agency has sought to place as much of the decision-making power as possible about its guaranteed loans into the hands of bankers.

SBA loans are limited to $500,000 and usually must be repaid within ten years. Businesses must not exceed certain size standards in terms of assets, annual sales, or number of employees to qualify for the SBA guarantee. In addition, an enterprise must have been turned down by three banks for standard loans before qualifying for an SBA-guaranteed loan.

Despite the rules and standards, though, the criteria for obtaining SBA loans aren't much different from obtaining regular bank loans. The SBA is primarily interested in the existence of business and personal collateral to protect the agency from default—and will avoid backing anything other than a 4/4 business. The agency, like banks and other lenders, has been known to foreclose on owners' homes which have been pledged as collateral, should their businesses default.

Once again, bank and SBA officials who must pass on SBA guarantees will be impressed by the existence of a business plan which accompanies the standard loan application forms. For young companies with assets of questionable worth, a well-done business plan can sometimes persuade officials to be more flexible in interpreting certain loan guidelines than otherwise.

In addition to the SBA, many states have in recent years begun making loans available to smaller businesses. Some of these programs involve state government guarantees of bank loans and others involve the use of state funds. As in the case of commercial loans and SBA-guaranteed loans, state agencies also seek collateral. Once again, an effective business plan can help smooth the way for successfully obtaining needed funds.

Don't Make Cold Calls

How should entrepreneurs go about obtaining the names of potential investors or lenders and approaching them? There's no easy answer to that question, as an exchange between two experts at an MIT Enterprise Forum session not long ago demonstrated.

An entrepreneur was describing his difficulties obtaining venture capital and wanted advice from panelists on the steps he might take. One panelist, an official of a large Boston-based venture capital firm, advised the entrepreneur to obtain the book mentioned earlier in this chapter, *Guide to Venture Capital Sources,* by Stanley Pratt. The entrepreneur should use the book to identify promising venture capital firms to which to send his company's business plan, the panelist suggested.

But a member of the audience, a banker with much experience assisting fledgling companies, immediately took issue with the panelist's recommendation. "When was the last time you financed a business whose plan you received over the transom?" he asked the panelist.

She thought for a few moments and, when she didn't answer, he asked, "Probably two years?" She agreed that was probably the case, adding that she wasn't simply suggesting the entrepreneur send the business plan out "blindly."

But the point was made. Cold calls may occasionally bring favorable responses, but more often than not they bring cold responses.

Implicit in the banker's argument was that entrepreneurs should make a serious effort to get an introduction of some sort before sending their business plans off to potential investors or lenders. The person making the introduction may vary according to the situation. In the case of informal investors, a friend or business associate is most often instrumental in bringing promising plans to their attention, according to William Wetzel, the University of New Hampshire researcher. Venture capitalists rely heavily on networks of bankers, accountants, and executive recruiters for referrals concerning potentially promising business plans.

The task for the entrepreneur, then, is not only to target specific informal investors, venture capitalists, or lenders, but also to find appropriate individuals to make the necessary preliminary introductions. That way, when the business plan arrives, it will be read by someone in a position of authority rather than discarded.

Thus, when an entrepreneur from western Massachusetts was seeking funding for his company, which produced a device that could turn wind power into electricity, he visited with the executive vice president he knew at a local bank. The banker realized that the venture didn't have enough collateral to cover the amount of financing it needed and thus wouldn't qualify for a loan, so he called a Boston venture capitalist he knew whose firm specialized in funding energy-related businesses.

The venture capitalist looked at the business plan right after he received it, made a date to meet with the company's management team, and eventually funded the business. Had the entrepreneur simply sent the business plan to the venture capitalist on his own, it may never have gotten beyond a low-level clerical person who screens business plans.

It's sometimes said that it's possible to meet anyone in the United States, including the President, through a maximum of three intermediaries. Entrepreneurs need to make use of all possible friends, acquaintances, business associates, lawyers, accountants, and others they know to get to potential investors and lenders.

Suppose an entrepreneur doesn't have a lot of contacts. That's certainly not unusual. He or she might be tempted to attend any of the various venture capital conferences springing up around the country. The conferences aren't unlike employment fairs or trade shows. In theory, entrepreneurs and investors get to know each other and, if they like what they see, they follow up after the conference.

In practice, though, that's a tough way for entrepreneurs to meet appropriate financiers. Although a few of these events have proven to be useful for providing places to meet, investors tend to be wary of such gatherings, figuring that only second-rate entrepreneurs will show up. After all, the reasoning goes, if the entrepreneurs and their business plans were so good, what would they be doing in a public setting looking for funds?

A more appropriate public setting might be the MIT Enterprise Forum. Even allowing for our favorable predisposition, it's safe to say that the MIT Enterprise Forum has earned the respect of local investors because the businesses which are permitted to present their business plans have been pre-screened. Moreover, the panelists who critique the plans are experienced and carefully chosen for their particular expertise concerning the business plans being presented.

Before making their own presentations, entrepreneurs can often make valuable contacts as well as learn much about business plans simply by attending MIT Enterprise Forum sessions. They usually attract accountants, lawyers, bankers, and investors who are well plugged into the local investment scene.

MIT Enterprise Forum sessions are now more accessible than ever. They've been established in a dozen cities, including Washington, New York, Chicago, Miami, Denver, Dallas, and Seattle. (A detailed description of the history and operations of the MIT Enterprise Forum is provided at the beginning of this book and a list of chapters at the back.)

What about Finders?

Because the process of preparing and circulating business plans is such an intimidating one, many entrepreneurs long to find a magical consultant who will handle it all for them. The fantasy usually has the entrepreneur answering a few of the consultant's questions and then waking up one morning a few weeks later to find several investors trying to outbid one another to back the venture.

Unfortunately, the fantasy is usually just that, a fantasy. The obstacle isn't as much trying to find a consultant to handle the writing and selling of the business plan—increasing numbers of consultants specialize in this area—as it is to sell financiers on the idea.

From the investors' or lenders' perspective, such consultants are essentially non-productive and a drain on a young company's limited resources. The consultants typically charge an hourly fee for helping write the business plan—$75 to $100 an hour isn't unusual—plus 5% or 6% of whatever funds they raise. To prospective financiers, such payments simply reduce the amount of money available for producing and marketing a new company's product or service.

Investors have one other concern when it comes to such consultants, or finders, as they're commonly known in the investment community. Investors worry that entrepreneurs who use finders to write and market the business plan are delegating two tasks the entrepreneurs should be handling themselves.

After all, if an outsider came up with the essentials of the marketing or production part of the plan, how closely will the entrepreneur stick to what's stated, investors wonder. And if the entrepreneur can't deal with selling the business plan in the investor marketplace, then how ably will he or she be able to sell the company in the consumer marketplace?

Investors' reasoning is not unlike the attitude many people adopt in evaluating load versus no-load mutual funds. The load funds command a fairly substantial up-front commission from investors—usually in the neighborhood of 3% to 8%. No-load funds have no such charge. Yet, there's no evidence that load and no-load funds differ substantially in performance. In that case, why not go with the no-load fund and save the commission?

As in many areas of consulting or brokering, there's no right or wrong answer. After all, we know many finders, and a number are extremely knowledgeable and experienced in the fine art of writing and selling business plans. And for entrepreneurs who write poorly, lack business experience, and have few connections, such consultants can sometimes be extremely helpful.

Entrepreneurs who feel strongly that they want to use such

a consultant's services should keep in mind, though, that finders vary quite widely in both their quality and the services they
offer. Some say they can fill the fantasy we described in the
opening of this section. They do it by using a cookie-cutter
approach to business plans. That is, they ask a few questions
and fill in the blanks of a master business plan, much like lawyers do in making standard wills and contracts.

We would advise entrepreneurs to steer clear of such
cookie-cutter operators. Writing a business plan, as we have
indicated previously, is much more an art and a process than it
is a simple fill-in-the-blanks writing assignment. Entrepreneurs
must make an assortment of judgment calls about the amount
of detail and research to include, if they're doing the plans
right.

Investors are extremely sophisticated in their ability to ana-
lyze business plans; those which haven't been custom-designed
will often stand out as such. Moreover, as we will discuss in
the next chapter, investors will expect to quiz entrepreneurs
whose business plans they like. Those entrepreneurs who
weren't part and parcel of the business-plan preparation process will likely encounter difficulties explaining and expanding
on the plan during the presentation process.

Thus, entrepreneurs intent on using a consultant should
take great care in locating and selecting one. They should rely
on recommendations of business experts whose judgments
they respect—accountants and bankers, for instance. Beyond
that, entrepreneurs should quiz the consultant closely on her
or his approach and be sure that they feel comfortable with
the person. References should be obtained and checked carefully. One reassuring sign is when the consultant appears to be
truly selective in deciding whether or not to work with individual entrepreneurs.

Owners should also be sure that the consultant involves

them heavily in the process, making them write and rewrite most of the plan before the consultant revises and edits it. And although finders' bread and butter are their contacts, entrepreneurs shouldn't be averse to lining up contacts of their own, in the event the finder encounters difficulties placing the plan.

As we indicated, finders usually charge an hourly rate for helping write the business plan, along with a percentage of the funds obtained. Like real estate agents, the finders often want exclusive rights to any deals negotiated within a certain period; a common arrangement is for a finder to receive a commission from any financing received by the enterprise for four months after the finder begins trying to line up funds as well as from any contacts the finder made during that period for financing received up to two years later.

Also important to keep in mind is that terms offered by finders are negotiable. It might be possible to increase the finder's commission for obtaining the required funds on favorable terms—say, by securing financing in return for 40% or less of the company—and reduce it for terms entrepreneurs regard as less favorable.

As investment funds become more widely available, the number and quality of such finders is sure to increase. There's no question that they have a role to play in the funding process, but for now, at least, entrepreneurs should play the finders game very close to the vest.

IN SUMMARY

Onoo oompleted, the business plan must be targeted toward investors or lenders likeliest to be interested in backing the venture. Investors want to back companies likeliest to exhibit annual growth exceeding 35%, while lenders extend credit to businesses with assets or orders on the books which can be pledged as collateral.

Among investor options are the following:

• Traditional venture capitalists, who invest $250,000 to $5 million, usually in companies at the 4/3 or 3/4 level minimum overall.

• Early-stage venture capital funds, which invest $50,000 to $250,000 in companies, usually at the 3/3 level.

• Investment bankers, who package fledgling businesses to go public so as to raise needed capital.

• Informal investors, who are the wealthy individuals who put up the $10,000 to $100,000 or more needed to advance 2/2 situations.

Among lender options are the following:

• Commercial lenders, including banks, finance companies, and others, which extend credit to companies at a 4/4 level.

• Government lenders, which include the SBA and state agencies and which also prefer 4/4 situations.

Entrepreneurs should seek to obtain introductions to potential investors and lenders before sending in their business plans. Professional consultants can assist in writing and circulating the business plan, but aren't always well received by financiers.

10

And Now It's Show Biz

After many long and frustrating months, you've completed your business plan. You've sent it to a few carefully chosen investors. You're waiting. Suddenly, there's a call from one of the investor groups. "We're interested. We'll be at your office next Tuesday at 10 a.m."

As a recent issue of the MIT Enterprise Forum's newsletter, *Forum Reporter,* put it in setting such a scene: "So now it's 'show biz.'" What's required of entrepreneurs? According to the newsletter, "A presentation . . . that will reinforce the initial interest and move things along, gaining momentum toward the desired conclusion."

Unfortunately, observed the *Forum Reporter,* "It is at this point that many negotiations falter—due to inadequate planning of the presentation—resulting in a disappointing performance that loses the investor's interest."

The newsletter offered this analysis: "The key question: how to put on a show that will present the company and its people favorably and honestly, using facts and projections that will stand careful scrutiny—without putting the audience into a state of catatonia. The solution: careful planning, critical review, plus rehearsals that are critiqued by both insiders and outsiders."

When potential investors call to "get together," it is the first indication entrepreneurs receive that their business plan is accomplishing its mission. Now it's up to the entrepreneurs to make the business plan, quite literally, come alive.

We noted in Chapter 2 that the two minutes investors spend reading a business plan's executive summary may be the most important two minutes in a young venture's life. If that's the case, then the thirty or forty minutes that entrepreneurs have to orally and visually present their company to investors may be the next most important time span in the business's life. This chapter explains how investors approach the presentation, how entrepreneurs should approach it, and how entrepreneurs can put on the best show posible.

Preparing for Marriage

The process of establishing investor-entrepreneur relations is similar in some ways to traditional courtship. The investor who reads through a business plan and becomes intrigued enough to reread it a few times isn't unlike the woman who goes out on a blind date and enjoys herself enough to accept a few subsequent dates. And when the investor decides that the time has come to meet the management team, it's as if the woman decides, after a few times out, that she's suddenly become serious and it's time to introduce the man to her parents.

Ignoring for now the sexist connotations of this analogy, the woman and her parents will be looking the man over as a potential husband and member of the family. How attractively—through dress, behavior, and conversation—does he present himself? What is his occupation? What are his long-term aspirations? Does he want children? What's his personality like? How empathetic is he? What are his manners like? Does he share some of their interests in terms of entertainment or hobbies? And on and on.

In other words, the man will be closely scrutinized for both tangible and intangible factors. So it will be with investors looking over entrepreneurs. The investors know they are embarking on a relationship which, if consummated, is closely akin to marriage. That is, the investor-entrepreneur relationship is a long-term one. Both sides will need to work hard to make it succeed. There will be inevitable crises which the two sides will need to resolve. And, like marriage, it is a lot easier relationship to get into than to get out of.

Among the tangible factors investors will want to consider are the following:

* How well prepared is the management team for making an oral presentation of the business plan?
* How clearly and coherently does the management team explain the venture's markets and products?
* How well do the entrepreneurs sell the company and its concept?
* Are the founders truly market-oriented or are they essentially technologists without enough regard for cash flow and profits?
* How well do the entrepreneurs sell themselves in terms of their experience and expertise?
* How quick are they on their feet in responding to investors' questions?

Among the intangible factors investors will be curious about are the following:

* What kind of integrity does the management team demonstrate?
* What's the appearance of the entrepreneurs and of their business office?

- What's the interpersonal "chemistry" between the investors and entrepreneurs?
- How receptive do the entrepreneurs appear to be to constructive criticism?
- How flexible is the management team in terms of accepting advice?

Entrepreneurs can assume that investors who meet with them will have sought to answer some of these questions in advance of the meeting. That is, the investors will likely have already begun their process of "due diligence." They will no doubt have done some preliminary research to check out the entrepreneurs' claims about the potential market, customers, competitors, and product.

In addition, the investors will probably have invested a few hundred dollars to hire a private investigator or detective agency to check on the entrepreneurs' business and personal backgrounds. Such a background investigation will involve such steps as interviewing previous employers (or investors), checking personal credit, and looking into medical histories of the founders.

The investors essentially want to learn as much as possible about the integrity and reliability of those to whom they will be handing over substantial amounts of money and with whom they will be involved in a long-term relationship. They want to know if the entrepreneurs have been involved in any questionable business activities, have used drugs, or have experienced disabling episodes of mental illness, among other issues.

Investors know from experience that such checks often turn up valuable information. In one situation investors learned that an entrepreneur they were considering backing had delayed in repaying his company's bank loan and had once issued a $50,000 bad check. Although those revelations didn't squelch the deal, they alerted the investors to demand certain terms and possible penalties for violation, which had the effect of making the entrepreneur more careful in his financial dealings than he was accustomed to being.

Entrepreneurs should also be aware that investors—venture capitalists in particular—are a closely knit community in many areas of the country and share information about businesses they consider backing. So if unfavorable information falls into the hands of one investor group, it may well spread quickly within the local investor community and perhaps even beyond.

It should be noted that unfavorable information which materializes about entrepreneurs isn't necessarily accurate information. A jealous former business colleague or a resentful neighbor can easily distort facts or even lie in response to an investigator's questions.

For that reason, we suggest that entrepreneurs consider asking a friendly outside party—a business owner or corporate official—to engage an investigative service to do a background check on themselves. That way, they will quickly determine if there is negative or derogatory information floating around that needs to be dealt with. And they will be prepared to confront issues and avoid negative surprises.

Entrepreneurs Have Rights, Too

Business founders tend to view the investment process entirely as a financial one. They become obsessed with obtaining the funds they're looking for at the lowest cost in terms of equity. The fact of the matter is that there's more to the investment process from the entrepreneur's viewpoint than simply obtaining funds.

To follow up on our courtship analogy earlier in this chapter, entrepreneurs are in an awkward position as the presentation time approaches. By virtue of having a company's business plan, potential investors in effect know many of the entrepreneurs' most intimate secrets. The entrepreneurs, in contrast, usually know very little about the investors. It's as if, just prior to the woman introducing her date to her parents, she provides them with a thorough briefing on his background and withholds from him much information about the parents' background, attitudes, health, likes, and dislikes.

Entrepreneurs in their quest for funds must keep in mind that they'll want to do some evaluating of their own both before and during their meetings with investors. Just as investors seek to find out as much as possible about any business they might back, in advance of meeting with the management team, so should entrepreneurs do some homework before the first get-together. Such inquiries should include checking venture capital directories and local professionals (bankers and accountants) to find out the names of other companies the investors have financed and, if possible, speak with principals of one or two of the companies.

This last task is a tricky one. Ideally, the other companies the investors have backed are in a similar industry and the possibility of finding an intermediary to arrange an introduction to the principals isn't as far-fetched as might at first appear. But failing that, entrepreneurs can call principals of other companies cold and explain the circumstances, requesting discretion. Responsible investors will consent to a "symmetrical" checkout. Bankers, accountants, and other professionals in frequent contact with investors may also be able to provide background information about particular investors.

What do entrepreneurs want to know about investors in advance of the actual meeting? First, they'll want to know about some tangibles. What markets and types of products particularly turn the investors on? And which turn them off? What special traits do the investors look for in the management team?

Entrepreneurs should also seek to learn something about the modus operandi of the investors. As we indicated in the previous chapter, investors come in all sizes, shapes, and flavors insofar as the types and sizes of ventures they'll finance. Investors also differ in the way they approach the investment process and the roles they will play in the follow-up relationship.

For instance, some investors are most comfortable being follow-on backers to a lead investor organization, which will put up the bulk of funds. Some investors insist on playing an active role in a company's decision making after funding, usually by having a representative on the board of directors. Other investors prefer to keep their distance from the venture after financing is completed.

Entrepreneurs should seek to determine the investors' usual approach to the investment process. It could be that the investors who express the first interest in a company will be follow-on backers; thus, even if they like the company, it will still be necessary to find a lead investor before the financing will be a reality.

Entrepreneurs should also try to find out about the kind of post-investment role investors like to play. Founders need not fear investors who like to be involved with each company they back. Indeed, because of their wide experience with young companies and the degree of specialization now common among investors, they can often provide important assistance to fledgling companies.

Not surprisingly, this kind of value added isn't free. Investors willing and able to offer specialized management guidance will likely also demand a larger chunk of the company than investors who are unwilling or unable to offer such assistance.

Because entrepreneurs tend to be independent and skeptical of outside assistance, they are often tempted to dismiss investor involvement as unnecessary meddling. Especially when such involvement carries a price tag.

We would caution entrepreneurs to take the availability of assistance quite seriously, since it might help them avoid marketing, production, and other blunders which are so common to young companies and which can be so dangerous early in a business's life. Indeed, those entrepreneurs lucky enough to have a choice between investors who have no inclination to provide assistance and those eager to be involved in the company, but who demand a higher equity price, are usually smart to choose the second option.

Next, entrepreneurs should try to learn about certain intangibles. What kind of reputation do the investors have for honesty and integrity? Do they make verbal promises which are conveniently forgotten later? What kinds of personalities and tastes do the investors have? If they're conservative, brie-and-chablis, classical music types, it won't do to regale them with off-color jokes and take them to the newest restaurant in town specializing in live rock or country-and-western music.

If answers to all these questions aren't forthcoming before the initial meeting with investors, it's appropriate to ask at least some of the questions during the meeting. The most important among those it's all right to inquire about are whether the investors tend to be lead or follow-on types and whether they like to be involved in advising the company after financing is completed. The answers to other questions, such as the investors' managerial likes and dislikes and negotiating style will likely become quickly apparent.

The more entrepreneurs know in advance about their potential suitors, the better prepared they can be during the face-to-face encounters.

Putting on the Show

The MIT Enterprise Forum provides entrepreneurs with an opportunity to present an abbreviated version of their oral presentation. They have twenty minutes to summarize their business plan, plus another five or ten minutes to respond to panelists' and audience comments.

Based on the presentations we see at the MIT Enterprise Forum, it's safe to say that many of the presentations that investors view aren't very impressive. It's not uncommon, after a presentation, for nearly everyone in the audience to be uncertain about what the company's product or service is or what its target market really consists of.

A fairly typical example was an entrepreneur seeking financing to produce a device which somehow helps items move more smoothly than otherwise on certain types of production lines. He started his presentation by dimming the lights so he could show slides which highlighted the company's product in action. Unfortunately, he didn't have a pointer to show the audience his company's product being used on the pictures of production lincs he showed. Then he had to skip over several slides because he didn't know their purpose. "We put this together rather quickly," he apologized, after wasting about half his twenty-minute allotment on such bungling. Just to add insult to injury, much of the panelists' and audience's time was spent questioning the entrepreneur as to what the company's product was supposed to do and how it differed from other products. "You don't seem to be able to explain the advantages of your product," observed one panelist.

Essentially, this entrepreneur and many others who make similarly incompetent presentations are blowing a big opportunity. However much investors may like the written business plan, they won't back entrepreneurs who can't stand up and coherently articulate where the company has been, where it is now, and where it is headed.

One Boston venture capitalist, in commenting on an entrepreneur's unimpressive performance at an MIT Enterprise Forum session, observed, "Sometimes our firm will be the first to see a group of founders, and we'll be so turned off by their presentation that we won't pursue the deal. Then five months later, we'll hear that they received funding from a top-notch venture capital firm. What happened is that the founders improved their presentation each time out, based on the questions they were hearing from the venture capitalists. After all, investors are not very original in their questions. After seeing three or four venture capital firms, entrepreneurs learn enough to put together a first-class presentation, so that the last group of venture capitalists is just bowled over."

Those entrepreneurs who get a second, third, and fourth chance to make their presentations are extremely fortunate—and rare. Because the venture capital community is so closely knit, word of a clumsy and inarticulate presentation may get around quickly. Thus, many founders discover too late that one poor presentation means that the ball game is over.

What are the elements of an effective presentation? We have delineated five, as follows:

1. *Set the tone appropriately.* One member of the management team, preferably the chief executive officer, should serve as master of ceremonies and be in charge of introducing the management team and making the presentation. The MC during the initial introductions can then offer a few words of back-

ground about each company official—perhaps noting a product development accomplishment or a well-known previous employer.

The MC should also ask any initial questions about the investors' possible role in the financing and subsequent management of the company. When it is clear that the investors are ready for the presentation, the MC should announce how long the presentation will take—thirty to forty minutes is appropriate—and invite the investors to interrupt with questions. Some investors won't interrupt at all, while others will interrupt continuously, stretching the presentation to one-and-a-half hours or more.

2. *Maintain eye contact with the investors.* More often than not, entrepreneurs at the MIT Enterprise Forum begin their presentations by turning down the lights and showing slides of their company's product being produced and used. When they've finished with the slides, the presenters commonly switch to showing viewgraphs of complex and difficult-to-read financial tables using an overhead projector. In some cases, the presenter reads from a prepared text as well.

We would argue against all these approaches—the slides, the viewgraphs, and the prepared texts—as counterproductive because they detract from the main goals of establishing personal rapport and building interest in the enterprise. Turning down the lights makes many people yawn automatically, as they subconsciously associate darkness with going to sleep. Similarly, faded and complex financial tables frustrate investors, because they must strain themselves to understand the data. And reading from prepared texts eliminates spontaneity and tends to be dull, if not soporific.

Most appropriate is for the presenter to maintain eye contact with the audience as he or she speaks, without notes or text. An easel with flip charts containing bulleted summaries of key points should be displayed as the speaker proceeds. Thus, instead of displaying the whole table of financial projections, just the projected sales, cost of sales, and margins might be noted.

The entrepreneur should feel free to address investors by name if their attention seems to be flagging. ("As you can see, Mr. Money, we will reach break-even at the beginning of year two.")

If for some reason it's more practical to use an overhead projector, be sure that the viewgraphs are clear and simple, with large letters that are easy to read. They should complement the presentation, not distract from it. In no case should typed pages be projected; they can't be read by the audience, they have too much detail, and they'll put investors to sleep.

3. *Emphasize the market, management team, and long-term goals.* Many presenters at the MIT Enterprise Forum spend the first ten or fifteen minutes of their presentation describing their company's product or service—what it does and how it works. Then, at the end of the talk, they offer a barebones explanation of the market size. This can be the kiss of death in trying to attract investment.

Just as the business plan should emphasize issues concerning the market, management team, and long-term goals of the company, so should the oral presentation. What is the rationale, based on the current and future state of the market, for the company's existence? What benefit will customers gain and how long is the payback period for the product or service? Exactly how will the company sell its product? What evidence is there of customer acceptance? What does the company want to be when it grows up?

As certain of these and other issues are dealt with, appro-

priate members of the management team should be intro-
duced and allowed three to five minutes to explain a key
segment of the company's approach. Each introduction should
be carefully constructed to emphasize the team member's past
experience and expertise. Then, the vice president, of sales,
for instance, can discuss the company's approach to distribut-
ing and selling the product. The vice president of finance can
discuss the financial projections and how they were arrived at.

Such discussions by members of the management team not
only convey important information about the company's situation and goals, they also reassure investors that the team exists
in more than name only. If only the chief executive speaks—
regardless of how he or she refers to other managers—investors immediately think "one-man band" and lose interest.

That was the case at a recent MIT Enterprise Forum session
at which the founder made the entire presentation; when he
was questioned by panelists about his team, he mentioned
how he had a vice president of sales and a vice president of
finance, but he didn't identify them by name. And as if to
reinforce the uneasiness panelists felt, he noted, "Of course, if
I could, I'd fill out the team by cloning myself five or six
times." At that point it was clear that the founder didn't take
well to sharing authority or responsibility. He clearly had
alienated a large segment of his audience.

The product or service can be described near the middle of
the presentation by the chief executive along with the vice
president of research and development or engineering. The
challenge for entrepreneurs is to resist the temptation to dwell
on the technicalities of the product or service. It's a difficult
temptation to resist, because the founders have usually devoted much of their time and energy to the development of
the product or service.

Most important is to emphasize the market, user benefit,

and how investment will grow and be returned to the investors, multiplied appropriately. Indeed, it's preferable to err on the side of devoting too little time to discussing the product or service than too much. If an insufficient amount of attention has been given to the product or service, investors will ask questions about it. But better to have satisfied their curiosity about the market, management team, and company goals first than to have regaled, and perhaps bored, them with discussion about what makes the product work.

4. *Demonstrate the product or service, if possible.* Much more than any verbal product description or slide projection, an actual demonstration of a product or service prototype will impress investors. A fledgling public relations agency might show some typical news releases, and a consulting firm might present a sample client report.

If the product is too large or the service too complex to demonstrate easily in an office, offer to take the investors to a place where it is operating, preferably in a customer's plant or offices. Thus, officials of a new temporary employment agency could show investors an office or plant where the venture's temps are working.

Two recent presentations to the MIT Enterprise Forum of office automation systems that allow colleagues and outside callers to leave telephone messages on computers suggest the importance of demonstrating the product or service. In the first presentation, the entrepreneurs brought their product along, installed in a computer, so that during the presentation they could phone various types of messages in and retrieve them to play back to the audience. Panelists and audience members were clearly impressed.

In the second case, the presenter simply described the product, which sounded similar to the first product. From the comments of panelists and audience members, though, it was clear that confusion existed about exactly what the company's product could and couldn't do. One panelist commented: "The uniqueness of your product is not clear. Who is buying this and why?"

Being able to demonstrate the product not only enables investors to understand it without having to endure a long and complicated explanation, it reassures them that the company is past the idea stage. Taking investors to a place where the product is being used accomplishes the same purpose but more effectively. When potential investors saw a venture's special product for improving detergent quality in use at a detergent manufacturing company, the venture had investment funds within three weeks.

5. *All top shows must be rehearsed.* Broadway shows are rehearsed first in private and then often in smaller cities such as Hartford or New Haven. When the show finally opens in the Big Apple, the performers have smoothed over or eliminated the rough spots and feel confident about their abilities. Major-league baseball teams do their rehearsing during spring training in Florida and Arizona.

Entrepreneurs who expect backing from experienced investors must similarly rehearse so as to emphasize their strengths and come across as seasoned professionals. That means going through the presentation several times in private and then going before a friendly audience—business associates, critical friends, or even a local drama expert, for some feedback. A professor from the drama department of a local college can be employed as a consultant.

Everything must be choreographed. If the investors are making an afternoon visit to the entrepreneurs' office, there should be soft drinks and coffee (coffee and donuts for the morning) available and a meeting room with proper lighting, air conditioning in summer, and general comforts. The office area shouldn't look like a paper factory after a cyclone, just as it shouldn't look so neat that it appears as if no work is done. But investors do want to see how entrepreneurs treat their own property as an indication of how they'll treat the investors' funds, so the office should look appropriately businesslike.

If you are doing the visiting, inquire about the general dimensions and layout of the meeting room. You should also determine whether any special equipment or other props should be brought along to demonstrate the company's product.

The actual presentation can be put into a summary of the desired script, so that each member of the management team winds up with an abstract idea of what he or she is to say. The team members can also decide in advance who will answer questions on particular subjects. Usually, it's best to allow the chief executive to field questions and decide which to answer himself or herself and which to parcel out.

The idea of all this preparation is to go as far as possible toward eliminating surprises. It's usually impossible to have everything under control. For instance, an investor may insist that a particular team member answer a certain question. Or investors may request that the product be demonstrated earlier in the presentation than the entrepreneurs planned to demonstrate it. But the better prepared the entrepreneurs are, the less likely that surprises will occur and the more likely the team members are to quickly adapt to the change in procedure.

What happens if, after all this, the investors are favorably impressed? Expect follow-up meetings and discussions.

Chances are the investors will want to spend some time simply getting to know the team members informally, over dinner or as part of an evening at a concert or some other entertainment. Spouses are often included in such affairs.

Entrepreneurs must avoid their inclination to become impatient with such seemingly slow-motion rituals. One Boston venture capitalist recalls inviting to dinner an entrepreneur whose business he was considering backing. The entrepreneur declined, saying he really didn't care much for social occasions. The courtship ended at that point, the venture capitalist recalls. "I like to get to know the people I'm backing," he observes. "If he didn't see the importance or have the time to get together in a social situation, then I don't want to become involved with him in an investment situation." And so the deal was off before it could actually begin.

Entrepreneurs who can successfully carry the game beyond the business plan into an effective presentation and follow-up relationship will likely find themselves suddenly in a situation where they're negotiating financing terms. At that point, they've joined the select group of 1% or less of business plans which wind up being funded by professional investors.

IN SUMMARY

Not only must entrepreneurs be able to present a convincing written case for funding, they must also be prepared to make a convincing oral case as well. Among the key considerations for entrepreneurs to keep in mind as they prepare for face-to-face meetings with potential investors are the following:

• The investor-entrepreneur relationship is similar in important respects to marriage. Investors will assess tangible factors such as the team's preparation and ability to sell the company as well as intangible factors such as the team's integrity and flexibility.

• Entrepreneurs must evaluate potential investors for more than simply the investment terms they might offer. Team members should assess in advance of getting together the kinds of situations potential investors prefer, their usual approach to the investment process, and whether they are likely to be lead or follow-on investors.

• Entrepreneurs must carefully rehearse their oral presentation. Among the elements of a successful presentation are having a master of ceremonies, maintaining eye contact with investors, emphasizing market and management-team expertise, and demonstrating the product or service.

If the entrepreneurs are guided by these principles, the probability of securing investment will be multiplied significantly.

MIT Enterprise Forum℠ Locations Program/Officer Directory 1984/85

MIT Enterprise Forum℠—Cambridge

MIT Alumni Center
77 Massachusetts Avenue
Cambridge, MA 02139
(617-253-8240)

MIT Enterprise Forum℠ of Chicago

P.O Box 350
Kenilworth, IL 60043
(312-256-4422)

MIT Enterprise Forum℠ of Colorado

c/o 7730 Sangre de Cristo
Littleton, CO 80127

Caltech/MIT Enterprise Forum℠ (Los Angeles)

Industrial Relations Center, 1-90
California Institute of Technology
Pasadena, CA 91125

University of Miami Venture Council/MIT Enterprise Forum^{SM}

School of Business Administration
University of Miami
Box 248027
Coral Gables, FL 33124
(305-284-4692)

MIT Enterprise Forum^{SM} **of New York**

MIT Alumni Center of New York
50 East 41st Street
New York, NY 10017
(212-532-8181)

MIT Enterprise Forum^{SM} **of the Northwest**

c/o James J. Battell
KIRO Television
Third Avenue and Broad Street
Seattle, WA 98121

MIT Enterprise Forum^{SM} **of Texas**

2727 Allen Parkway, 17th Floor
Houston, TX 77019
(713-521-2789)

MIT Enterprise Forum^{SM} **of Washington/Baltimore**

PO. Box 33079
Washington, DC 20033-0079
(301-656-96260)

Index